PITCHING TO THE STAR

And Other Short Plays

BY DONALD MARGULIES

★

★

DRAMATISTS
PLAY SERVICE
INC.

PITCHING TO THE STAR AND OTHER SHORT PLAYS
Copyright © 1993, Donald Margulies

All Rights Reserved

SPECIAL NOTE

SPECIAL NOTE ON SONGS AND RECORDINGS

TABLE OF CONTENTS

PITCHING TO THE STAR 5

L.A. 37

SPACE 51

WOMEN IN MOTION 59

ZIMMER 79

PITCHING TO
THE STAR

PITCHING TO THE STAR was first presented at the West Bank Cafe Downstairs Theatre Bar (Lewis Black and Rand Foerster, Artistic Directors), in New York City, on March 20, 1990. It was directed by Rand Foerster. The cast was as follows:

DICK ....Lewis Black
PETER ....Robert Sean Leonard
LAURI ....Mary Kane
DENA ....Kathryn Rossetter
VOICES OF JENNIFER AND TYNE....................Lynn Chausow

CHARACTERS

PETER ROSENTHAL, 32, the writer
DICK FELDMAN, 40s, the producer
DENA STRAWBRIDGE, 40s, the star
LAURI RICHARDS, 28, the D-Girl
VOICE OF JENNIFER, 30s, Dick's secretary
VOICE OF TYNE, 10, Dick's daughter

SETTING

The office of Dick Feldman at his home in Sherman Oaks, California. The present.

Primarily, the office furnishings are white. Cans of Diet Coke are on the Santa Fe-style coffee table. A voice-activated intercom/speaker is prominently placed on the rear wall.

PITCHING TO THE STAR

DICK. It's a courtesy thing.

PETER. Uh huh.

DICK. No big deal. What, you're scared?

PETER. No.

DICK. You're *nervous*? *(To Lauri.)* Look at him. *(Lauri laughs; to Peter.)* Dena *Straw*bridge, you're *nervous*?

PETER. No, I just didn't expect ...

DICK. She's the *star*. So *what*? Big fucking deal. People *know* her? She's well-known? So?

PETER. I didn't think (today) I'd ...

DICK. People know her *face*? So? She's a has-been. A druggie. Her tits sag. Boy, this celebrity shit really impresses you, doesn't it.

PETER. *(A little p.o.'ed.)* No, it's just —

DICK. You're *really* new in town, aren't you.

PETER. — I didn't think I'd have to *pitch* ...

DICK. I'm *teasing* you. Hey. We want to *include* her a little bit, that's all. Make her feel, *you* know, like a star, important. So you pitch the pilot to her. Nothing to it. She likes the pitch?, she doesn't like it?: Same difference. You don't have to sell *her*, you sold *us*. Get it?

PETER. Uh huh.

DICK. You're *ours*, not *hers*. Remember that. You don't have to *deal* with her, let *me* deal with her. You just be nice. Be pleasant. Be cute. You *are* cute. She'll like you. Just be cute, you'll see. Be yourself. She'll love you. It's not what you *say* (you understand?), it's not what you *pitch*. Let her think we

9

care what she thinks. (That's what today is about.) She says something? Go: "Uh *huh*, let me think about that." She'll love you for life. Don't write it *down* even, just: "Uh *huh*." Like: "What an interesting idea. Gee, I must give that some thought, Dena, thank you." Guarantee she won't remember what she said thirty seconds later but you made a friend for life. You were pleasant. You didn't show an attitude. You don't *want* to be her friend. Remember that. I'm talking purposes of the show solely. She's the star. You don't fuck with a star, so to speak. She, in her mind, is apart from the rest of the world. She's a star. Stars don't know *how* to be a friend. They don't *have* friends. They're suspicious of everyone. They don't *like* people. They're ambivalent about their success. They don't know what they did to *deserve* it, which makes them very suspicious of people. With good reason when you think about it: People *want* things from stars. So, consequently, as a result, they're suspicious, lonely, deeply fucked-up people. Remember: you don't *want* to be her friend. You don't need *her*. She needs *you*. *Fuck* her. *(Calls.)* Jennifer? Jen?

JENNIFER'S VOICE.   *(Over intercom.)* Yes, Dick?

DICK.   What time is it?

JENNIFER'S VOICE.   Twelve-twenty, Dick.

DICK.   *What* time?

JENNIFER'S VOICE.   Twenty after twelve. *(Lauri shows Dick her watch.)*

DICK.   She's late. *Star* shit. Already it's starting. I'm telling you, she pulls that shit with *me* ...

PETER.   So she knows about the style of the show? She knows how we want to shoot it?

DICK.   Bubbie, what did I just finish saying? She doesn't know shit.

LAURI.   I think what Peter's asking —

DICK.   It's not like we have to con*sult* with her. We're not looking for her ap*prov*al.

PETER.   I mean, she knows we're talking about a one-camera film show?

DICK.   We'll get you as many cameras as you want.

PETER.   I only want one.

DICK. So we'll get you one. Jesus Christ. What are you so worried about? *(To Lauri.)* You ever see such a worrier? *(Lauri laughs.)*

PETER. I'm not worried. I just want to make sure —

DICK. What, what's the problem here?

PETER. Nothing. I just want to make sure.... Remember the very first conversation we had? I told you I wasn't interested in writing a three-camera sitcom? I'm only interested in writing a half-hour film.

LAURI. Yes, Peter feels very strongly about this, Dick.

DICK. Huh?

LAURI. Peter feels —

DICK. *(To Peter.)* What are you suggesting?

PETER. I'm not suggesting anything. I just want your assurance that —

DICK. And you have it. Period. The End. I don't understand the problem here.

PETER. Dick, there's no problem. Don't misconstrue my concern.

DICK. Nobody's misconstruing anybody.

LAURI. I think what Peter is saying —

PETER. What if — just listen to me a second — indulge me, okay? — What if we pitch the show to Dena Strawbridge and she loves it, and then we say, "By the way, this is a film show," and she says, "Oh, sorry, I don't want to do a film show." What do we do?

DICK. We dump her.

PETER. Really?

DICK. She doesn't want to do it our way? Absolutely. We dump her. "Sorry, Dena," whatever. "Ah, that's too bad, we want to go for something else." That's all there is to it.

PETER. Yeah?

DICK. You worried about getting this on the air? Write it good, bubbie, it'll get on the air, Dena Strawbridge or no Dena Strawbridge. There are hundreds of has-been Dena Strawbridges out there. We can always find a new star. This is Los Angeles.

PETER. Okay.

DICK. Hundreds. Are you fucking kidding me? Look through the Players Guide. People you thought died horribly long ago are in there, waiting for a shot like this, are you kidding?

PETER. Okay. Good.

DICK. All right? You feel better now?

PETER. Yeah.

DICK. Good. Thank God. *(To Lauri.)* New York playwrights, I'm telling *you* ... *(She laughs. He claps his hands together; to Peter.)* All right, boychick, let's hear it.

PETER. You mean *now?*

DICK. Yeah, run it by me.

PETER. Oh, okay.

DICK. What, you don't wanna?

PETER. No, I didn't know we were gonna ...

DICK. We're going in to the network tomorrow, bubbie, we're not gonna walk in *cold.* You didn't think we were just gonna walk in ...

PETER. No. I don't know ... *(Making light of it.)* I just got here from the *airport,* Dick. I mean, I haven't even had a chance to take a *shower.*

DICK. *(Kibitzing, sort of.)* What, you're gonna be *sensitive?*

PETER. No, I'm kidding ...

DICK. You can't pitch if you smell? Huh? You're worried you smell?

PETER. I'm *kidding* ...

DICK. We're *friends* here. *(To Lauri.)* Right?

LAURI. Absolutely.

DICK. We're *friends.* We don't *care* you smell. I'm *teasing* you. *(To Lauri.)* Look at him, look how sensitive ...

PETER. Who's sensi — Okay. So.... You mind if I refer to my notes?

DICK. Go head.

PETER. I promise tomorrow I'll be more "up." I'll be rested, I'll be bathed ...

DICK. *(To Lauri.)* Boy, this guy is a real (whatayacallit?) a cleanliness freak or something. *(Lauri laughs.)* A shower fetishist.

PETER.   I'm kidding ...

DICK.   I *know* you're kidding, bubbie, I *know*. *I'm* kidding. *(To Lauri.)* He's stalling. Look at how he's stalling.

PETER.   *(Launching into the pitch.)* Okay. *Working Mom.*

DICK.   What is this, a *book* report? *(To Lauri, who laughs.)* He's doing a book report. *(To Peter.)* *Only kidding.* Go head. Great so far, I love it. I love that title. *(To Lauri.)* Don't *you?*

LAURI.   Great title.

DICK.   *(To Peter.)* Go head. Sorry. No more interruptions.

PETER.   Okay. So —

DICK.   *(Calls.)* Jen?

JENNIFER'S VOICE.   Yes, Dick?

DICK.   *(Calls.)* Hold all calls.

JENNIFER'S VOICE.   I am, Dick.

DICK.   *(To Peter.)* All yours, pal.

PETER.   Okay, here we go. *(Clears throat.)* What we hope to do with *Working Mom,* what we hope to *accomplish,* is to explore, in very real terms, what it means to be a single, working-class working mother today. *(Dick takes the notes out of Peter's hands, looks them over.)*

DICK.   What *is* this?

PETER.   These are the notes I sent you.

DICK.   What notes?

PETER.   I FedExed them to you two weeks ago. I don't have a FAX, remember? You wanted them as quickly as possible.

DICK.   How come *I* never saw these notes?

LAURI.   I gave them to you, Dick. Remember?

DICK.   All I can say is I never saw these notes.

LAURI.   I *gave* them to you.

DICK.   And I'm telling you I never saw them.

LAURI.   They were right on your desk. I *put* them on your desk.

DICK.   And I never *saw* them, okay? I never *saw* them. *(Hands them back to Peter.)* You should've gotten feedback on this.

PETER.   When I didn't hear from you, I assumed they were okay.

DICK.   Never assume. I'm saying I'm sorry. The error occurred in this office.

LAURI. I put them on your desk, Dick.

DICK. *(To Peter.)* Go on.

PETER. Um ... to explore, in very real terms —

DICK. I'm not sure about this "explore" shit ...

PETER. No?

DICK. Sounds so ... surgical. This is *comedy,* man.

PETER. I know. I'm just trying to ...

DICK. You do this at the network (I'll be perfectly honest with you).... You do this at the network tomorrow, you might as well hand out pillows and blankies and tuck everybody in.

PETER. I said I'll have more energy tomorrow.

DICK. Fuck energy. Excuse me. I'm not talking energy or no energy. *The pitch has got to entertain.* Believe me. I've been doing this a lot longer than you have.

PETER. I know ...

DICK. If you don't grab them from the word go ...

LAURI. It's true.

DICK. *(To Lauri.)* Am I right?

LAURI. Absolutely. It has to —

DICK. This is key. *You have to make it sound like fun.* These guys don't know. You think they know shit? You have to show them *the potential for fun.* They need to know it's okay to enjoy themselves. You need to smile.

PETER. Smile?

DICK. Yeah. You look like you're sitting shiva.

PETER. I do? I'm sorry.

DICK. Hey. That's okay. That's what I'm here for. That's what today is about. These are things to keep in mind. Go on.

PETER. *(Continuing.)* Dena Flanders was a junior at Atlantic City High when she got pregnant for the first time. Her boyfriend, Paulie Vanzetti, married her and, even though they had two more kids, Paulie never could stop gambling and chasing cocktail waitresses. Dena's finally had it. She moves herself and her kids into her mother's house. All she wants is to get her life back on track. So, with the help of her tart-tongued mother (Olympia Dukakis), Dena takes night classes

14

to finish her high school degree. In the pilot, she gets a job as a paralegal in the storefront office of a crusty old leftie attorney named Al Sapirstein (Jerry Stiller).

DICK. Wait a second.

PETER. Yeah?

DICK. Pete. Hold it. *(Pause.)* You know that *play* of yours?

PETER. Which one?

DICK. The one I flipped over. The Jewish guy?

PETER. *Shabbos Goy?*

DICK. *Shabbos Boy,* that's right.

PETER. *Goy.*

LAURI. *Goy,* Dick.

DICK. Funny play. You had some scenes in there ...

PETER. Thank you.

DICK. You're a funny guy.

PETER. Thanks.

DICK. *(To Lauri.)* Isn't he a funny guy?

LAURI. Oh, God, are you kidding?

DICK. Very funny guy. And funny is money. *(To Lauri.)* No?

LAURI. Definitely.

DICK. *(To Peter.)* Let me tell *you:* Funny is money, my friend, and you are funny.

PETER. Well, thanks.

DICK. When I discovered that script of yours.... Howling! I was howling!

PETER. Really?

DICK. Uh! Funny funny stuff.

PETER. Thanks.

DICK. *Now:* you know how you wrote in your play?

PETER. Yeah...? What.

DICK. You know how *funny* you wrote?

PETER. Yeah...?

DICK. Do that here.

PETER. What.

DICK. Do that *here.* Be *funny.* Write funny. This isn't funny.

PETER. It may not *sound* funny ...

DICK. No. This is not funny.

PETER. When I *write* it ...

DICK. *(To Lauri.)* You think this is funny?

LAURI. Well I understand what he's —

DICK. No. It's not. Pete. Listen to me. You don't understand. Make this funny. What you've got *here* (believe me, I know what I'm talking about), it isn't funny. Plain and simple. No matter how you cut it. When you write it (believe me), it's gonna suck. Just think of your play. I read it. I know what you can do. Do what you did there.

TYNE'S VOICE. *(Over intercom.)* Daddy?

DICK. You can do it, Pete. *(Calls.)* Yes, baby.

TYNE'S VOICE. Daddy, Consuelo says I can't have Mrs. Fields. She says it's for supper.

DICK. It *is* for supper, Tyney. For coffee after. *(A beat.)* Tyne? *(He listens; she's gone; he takes off shoes, lays down on sofa.)* So, *good* so far. Let's hear the pilot. Pitch me the pilot.

PETER. Okay. So. The opening. I thought it would be fun if we opened with sort of a parody of that great sweeping pan of the Statue of Liberty that opens *Working Girl?* Remember the opening of *Working Girl?*

LAURI. Uh huh.

PETER. Well, I thought what we could do for *Working MOM* is the camera swoops really dramatically around the statue and then, instead of heading over to the Manhattan skyline, it ends up in New Jersey.

LAURI. Ooo. Nice. Isn't that nice, Dick?

PETER. *You* know, kind of working-class, industrial New Jersey. Refineries, highways, smog sunset. So there's a kind of irony there, from the word go, that tells us that this isn't gonna be another glossy single-working-mother kind of show. The irony is you think —

DICK. Wait wait wait. "Irony?" *(To Lauri.)* He's an intellectual. *(She laughs.)* Intellectuals (what can I tell you?), they love "irony." *(She laughs even more.)* I don't give a *shit* "irony."

PETER. I was just —

DICK. Excuse me. You pushed a button. I'm very emotional about this. You pushed a — there it goes.... You will learn this about me, Peter. Ask anybody who's worked with me. They will tell you the same: I do not bullshit. *(To Lauri; meaning,*

16

True?) Huh?

LAURI.   It's true.

DICK.   *(To Peter.)* Hey, I don't mean to blow you away.

PETER.   No, I'm all right ...

DICK.   *(To Lauri.)* He's looking at me like God knows ... *(To Peter.)* I'm your *friend* for telling you this. I know you're just off the plane so to speak. You're new in this town. Save your "irony" for the *stage.* Okay? (I'm about to save you a lot of grief.) Save it for the *theater.* That's all I have to say on the subject. Period, end quote. I don't bullshit people I like, I have *respect* for. *(To Lauri.)* Am I right?

LAURI.   Oh, absolutely.

DICK.   I don't have time for irony. Give me a story. Tell me a good story, I'm happy. That's all I ask: Give me a good story. Whatever happened to stories? Hm? Remember stories? Bubbeleh, this is what I'm telling you. We gotta clear your brain of that shit. We gotta vacuum it out. Simple stories, Peter. Where a cow is a cow·for a change. Boy meets girl. Yeah. No symbols. No irony. One thing doesn't mean another. Who wants to sit there (no really now), who wants to have to *sit* there and *work* and figure it out? "Oh, I get it: the so-and-so really means the *Holocaust.*" "Child abuse." Fill in the blank. Fuck it. Life is too short for irony. Please. Tell me the fucking story. *This* happens, then *this* happens, then *this* happens, so-on and so-forth. People after a hard day, they do not want to have to put on their thinking caps. *(Getting up, unzipping his fly.)* These are important lessons in this town, pal ... I swear one day you're gonna thank me. *(To Lauri.)* Look at him, he hates me. *(Lauri laughs.)* Fucking Diet Cokes ... *(While reaching into his fly, Dick exits to the bathroom. A beat.)*

LAURI.   You know Dick's never done TV before.

PETER.   What do you mean?

LAURI.   He's done *movies.*

PETER.   Oh, yeah, I know.

LAURI.   He had that one Tom Cruise thing, he got this deal as a result.

PETER.   Uh huh.

LAURI.   Sure, he was kicking around for years (who hasn't).

PETER. Uh huh.

LAURI. But the truth is ... when it comes to television...?

PETER. Yeah...?

LAURI. He doesn't know the first thing.

PETER. Oh, really.

LAURI. Not a thing. It's embarrassing. I *work* for this guy. I *work* for him. We go into these meetings at the network?

PETER. Yeah...?

LAURI. And it's like *unbelievable*.

PETER. Huh. *(Meaning, How do you like that?)*

LAURI. The guy. Doesn't. Know. The business. Television, I mean. Okay, so he had a hit movie. A lot of people have hit movies, doesn't make them experts in *television*. What does *he* know about *television*? He thinks he knows how to put together a *series*? It's a joke. I'm saving his ass all over town. I'm covering for him. I have to call the network after we meet with them?

PETER. Yeah...?

LAURI. To like patch-up for all the schmucky things he said? It's a joke. I was instrumental in *Charles in Charge* — *before* it went into syndication! I was *there*, learning, paying my dues, seeing how it's done. What does *Dick* know? Do you think he knows good material when he sees it? I have to *tell* him what's good. I have to *find* what's good (but that's not enough). *I have to get him to read it.* A writer doesn't *exist* out here until he's read. They don't know New York theater. I really had to fight for you, you know.

PETER. Oh, yeah? How do you mean?

LAURI. *I'm* the one who kept on pushing your play on him.

PETER. Well, thank you.

LAURI. These people don't read. They do *not* read. I was in Theater, you know.

PETER. Oh, yeah? Where'd you go to school?

LAURI. B.U.?

PETER. Uh huh.

LAURI. I always felt that we could really break ground with *Working Mom*, we could really do some important television — *if* we found the right writer for the pilot. Someone who's fresh and doesn't know all the sitcom tricks. We wanted you because you *don't* know the formula. You *don't* know the tricks. We wanted *grit* and humor *and* ethnicity, *authenticity*. You've got it all.

PETER. Thanks.

LAURI. You *do*. "Peter Rosenthal is who we want for *Working Mom*," I said. No, "Peter Rosenthal is who we *need*. If we don't get Peter Rosenthal — and he's very hot right now (this is what I told him) — if we don't *nab* him (and if we don't, we're idiots), if we don't fly him out here *right away*, then I ask you: My God, what are we all doing here?" *(Grasps his wrist; confidentially.)* Peter?

PETER. Yes, Lauri?

LAURI. Feel free to call me any time. You have my home number?

PETER. Yeah, I think you ...

LAURI. Any time.

PETER. You wrote it on your card.

LAURI. You're gonna need someone to talk to out here.

PETER. I appreciate that, Lauri, but I have friends ...

LAURI. No, I mean, these things can get pretty intense. Development, I mean. It can get dirty. You can get hurt if you don't watch out.

PETER. Thanks, Lauri.

LAURI. Hey, I feel responsible. I'm the one who got you out here. We have to protect writers like you. Do you know how *rare* it is to find a writer like you? I *cherish* writers. Writers are all we have. Really, when you think about it. Promise you'll call me.

PETER. I promise.

LAURI. Peter, you have *such* a unique comic *voice*, I can't tell you.

PETER. Thank you.

LAURI. No, thank *you*. You have no idea how many scripts I read. And it's all shit. Then to discover someone like you?! It's like: "Oh, yeah, right, *this* is why I want to produce. *This* is why I came out here." *(The toilet flushes. Dick returns.)*

DICK. What's this?

LAURI. Nothing. I was just telling Peter what a unique voice we think he has.

DICK. Oh, yeah. Really unique. So, where are we?

JENNIFER'S VOICE. Dena's here, Dick.

DICK. In the house or on her way?

JENNIFER'S VOICE. *Here.*

DICK. Shit.

LAURI. *(To Peter.)* Don't worry. *(Dena Strawbridge, early 40s, brittle, nervous, enters.)*

DENA. Hi. Sorry. I was at Pritikin.

DICK. Hey. Dena. There's my girl. *(He hugs her.)* Oh, man, so good to see you.

DENA. Good to see you, too.

DICK. You're looking sensational.

DENA. Yeah? Oh ...

DICK. *(To Lauri.)* Doesn't she look — ?

LAURI. Mm, yes!

DENA. Thank you. Do I know you?

DICK. My development exec, Lauri Richards?

DENA. Oh, hi.

LAURI. Hello. Really nice to meet you finally.

DENA. Thank you.

DICK. And, Dena? Remember that *terrific* young writer we told you about? From New York?

DENA. Yes!

DICK. This is Peter Rosenthal. From New York.

PETER. Hi. Nice to meet you.

DENA. Thank you. Wow. Really really nice to meet you, too ...

DICK. So! We were just pitching, the three of us.

DENA. Oh, yeah?

DICK. Sounds great.

DENA. Yeah?

DICK. Uh! You're gonna love it.

DENA. Oo! I can't wait. *(Grasping Dick's hand.) God,* am I glad we're working together ... *(He hugs her again.)*

DICK. Me, too. Didn't I tell you we *would* one day?

DENA. I am so so excited about this project. You mind if

I eat? *(She takes out her lunch.)*

DICK. No. Eat. What is that?

DENA. Oh, I'm on macro. It's great. You ever do it?

DICK. No.

DENA. Oh, it's great. I'm keeping my weight down, I'm more regular than I've ever been in my entire life.... It's great. Really. You should try it. I'll give you my nutritionist's number. He's fabulous. Oh! I have regards for you!

DICK. Oh, yeah? From who?

DENA. Joel Kaplan?

DICK. Joel Kaplan, no shit! How do you know Joel?

DENA. He produced my miniseries.

DICK. No kidding, is that so?

DENA. Yeah, and he's looking really good. Have you seen him lately?

DICK. He's had a hell of a time.

DENA. I know, but he's looking great. I just ran into him at Pritikin. He lost something like fifty pounds.

DICK. No kidding. Good for him. *(To Peter and Lauri.)* This guy was a fucking fat pig.

DENA. He's seeing Leonard, too. My nutritionist. Remind me to give you his number, you will love him.

DICK. Gee, I really should give Joel a call.... Where *is* he now?

DENA. Warners.

DICK. I thought he was at Universal.

DENA. That deal ran out. He got an even better deal at Warners. An *incredible* deal. And he looks really really great.

DICK. *(Calls.)* Jennifer?

JENNIFER'S VOICE. Yes, Dick?

DICK. *(Calls.)* Put Joel Kaplan on my call list? *(To Dena.)* Warners?

DENA. Uh huh.

DICK. *(Calls.)* He's at Warners. *(To Dena.)* Is he clean now, Joel?

DENA. Oh, yeah. You should see him.

DICK. I heard he had his nose redone.

DENA. Oh, yeah, he was in big big trouble. He was killing

21

himself.

DICK.   I didn't know it got so bad.

DENA.   The man was killing himself.

DICK.   Jeez ... *(To Peter.)* Joel Kaplan? You know him?

PETER.   No.

DICK.   Biggest asshole alive.

DENA.   Well ... he did a great job on my miniseries.

DICK.   Good.

DENA.   A super super job. Considering what he was going through.

DICK.   I'm glad he came through for you, Dena. I'm truly glad to hear that.

DENA.   Absolutely terrific.

DICK.   I'm an asshole: Tell me the name again?

DENA.   *The Deadly Weekend of Marilyn Monroe?*

DICK.   Oh, of course!

LAURI.   Oh, yes!

DICK.   I *am* an asshole! That was supposed to be ...

DENA.   I know.

DICK.   *(To Lauri.)* Did you see that?

LAURI.   No, I was in the hospital for my lumpectomy.

DICK.   We heard that was terrific! *(To Lauri.)* Didn't we hear that was terrific?

LAURI.   Oh, yes! Everybody was —

DENA.   It won me my Emmy nomination so I guess it must've been pretty —

DICK.   Yeah, congratulations on that!

LAURI and PETER.   Congratulations.

DENA.   *Thank* you.

DICK.   Did you win it?, I forget.

DENA.   No, no. Katharine Hepburn got it that year. But, I tell you, I was so honored just to be *nominated* with that lady.

LAURI.   Hm, yeah.

DICK.   Wow. Now I want to see it.

DENA.   I was so frigging proud. A role like that doesn't come along very often for a woman, let's face it. I got to do everything. The Bobby Kennedy scenes? I mean, between takes Marty Sheen had to *hold* me, that's how much I was

22

shaking ...

LAURI. Wow.

DICK. Shit, I really want to see this ... *(Calls.)* Jen?

JENNIFER'S VOICE. Yes, Dick.

DICK. Call the agency, see if they can get us a copy —

DENA. No, you don't have to do that ...

DICK. — of Dena's miniseries, *Deadly* ...

DENA. *Weekend of Marilyn Monroe.*

DICK. The Marilyn Monroe thing.

DENA. You really don't —

DICK. Tell them to messenger it over —

DENA. Dick, you really don't have to do that ... *(To Lauri.)* What a crazy nut. *(Lauri nods.)*

DICK. *(Overlap.)* — I want to look at it tonight.

DENA. You *don't* have to do this on my account.

DICK. I *want* to. Are you kidding? It'll be fun.

DENA. Well, good.

JENNIFER'S VOICE. Dick?

DICK. *(Calls.)* Yeah, Jen.

JENNIFER'S VOICE. I've got Joel Kaplan for you.

DICK. *(Calls.)* Joel Ka—? Who called who? *(To others.)* Isn't this freaky?

JENNIFER'S VOICE. You told me to get him.

DICK. *(Calls.)* I said put him on my *list*, Jennifer.

JENNIFER'S VOICE. Oh, I thought ...

DICK. *(Calls.)* Uh, look ... I said on my list ...

JENNIFER'S VOICE. Sorry, Dick ... I've *got* him ... *(A beat.)* What do you want me to do with him?

DICK. Tell him I'll have to get back to him. I'm in a meeting.

JENNIFER'S VOICE. Okay. Sorry, Dick.

DICK. *(Calls.)* Yeah. *(To others.)* Jesus. Do you believe her? She can be such a flake sometimes. *Now.* This *guy....* *(Meaning Peter.)* Are we lucky! This *boy....* *How* old are you?

PETER. 32.

DICK. Nah. You are not ...

PETER. Yes, I am.

DICK. You look 25, 26.

PETER.   I'm 32, though, believe me.

DICK.   Doesn't he look 25?

DENA.   Yeah, he does.

DICK.   25, 27 *maybe* ...

PETER.   No, I'm 32.

DICK.   You could pass. Easy. Lie. Fib. Tell people you're 25, they'll eat it up.

PETER.   But I'm not.

DICK.   Fib, I said. People out here, everybody's very impressed with how young you are. Everybody loves a prodigy. Say you're 25, mark my words. — *Anyhow* ... this *guy* ... this *boy* ... wrote a *play* ... ran in New *York* ... (Joe *Papp* produced this play).

DENA.   *(With interest.)* Uh huh?

DICK.   This *play* ... *Shabbos Boy* ... I'm telling you ... had me peeing in my pants. *(To Lauri.)* Right?

LAURI.   It did.

DICK.   Peeing! On the floor!

DENA.   Really?

DICK.   In my pants! *(To Lauri.)* Tell her.

LAURI.   It's true.

DENA.   Oh, how great!

DICK.   Funny, funny play.

PETER.   Thanks, Dick.

DICK.   Funny is money. I keep telling him that, he doesn't believe me.

PETER.   I believe you.

DICK.   He doesn't believe me. He thinks I'm *lying* he can be a gold mine out here.

PETER.   I believe you.

DICK.   There's a scene he's got in this play, Dena ...

DENA.   Yeah?

DICK.   Dena, this *scene* ... with the mother?

PETER.   The grandmother, actually.

DICK.   Huh?

PETER.   You mean with the grandmother? You told me ...

DICK.   The mother, the grandmother, whatever.... Anyhow, he's yelling at her about his bris? *(To Dena.)* Circumcision. You

24

know, when they *perform* it, the people, they throw a party ...

DENA. Oh, yeah, I know some people who did that ...

DICK. Anyhow, he's yelling, "How could you do something like that to me!"

DENA. Oh, how funny.

DICK. And she *sits* there. She *sits* there, the mother, the grandmother, and she doesn't say a word!

PETER. Oh, you mean the stroke scene?

DICK. What?

PETER. The stroke scene. The grandmother's had a stroke. That's why she doesn't say anything.

DICK. *(Thinks he's kidding.)* Nahhh ...

PETER. Yes! She's had a stroke and he doesn't realize it. That's what the scene is about.

DICK. Oh, you mean the *stroke* scene! Sure! Oh, yeah, of course. Well, the point is (whatever): a riot. The *play* is a riot.

DENA. What's the name of it again?

PETER. *Shabbos Goy.*

DICK. *Shabbos Boy.*

PETER. *Shabbos Goy.*

DICK. *Goy?* I thought *Boy.*

PETER. No.

DENA. What does it mean? I mean, I don't know Jewish.

PETER. A shabbos goy is a non-Jew hired by Orthodox Jews to do little chores ... like lighting the stove, turning on the electricity.... Orthodox Jews aren't allowed to do certain things on the sabbath. Saturday. That's what "shabbos" means: Saturday.

DENA. Oh! *I* get it.

DICK. That's a good title.

PETER. Thanks.

DICK. I mean, you should've called it that: *Shabbos Goy* not *Boy.*

PETER. I did.

DICK. Wait ... you did or you didn't?

LAURI. Dick? The name of the play *is Shabbos Goy.*

DICK.   *Shabbos Goy* has irony — I mean, it, uh, has more *meaning.*

PETER.   I agree. That's why I called it that.

DICK.   The copy we read ... I could swear it said "Boy." *(Calls.)* Jen? Jennifer?

JENNIFER'S VOICE.   Yes, Dick.

DICK.   Bring in a copy of Peter's play?

JENNIFER'S VOICE.   *Shabbos Goy?*

DICK.   Uh, never mind.

DENA.   So, what's it about, your play?

PETER.   It's a comedy, I guess. About assimilation.

DENA.   Uh huh. Neat. A comedy, huh? Isn't that kind of a tough subject?

PETER.   Well ...

DENA.   I mean, considering what's going on?

PETER.   *(A beat.)* What do you mean exactly?

DENA.   I mean, *you* know, South Africa.

PETER.   South Africa?

DENA.   *You* know, what's going on over there with that.

PETER.   *(A beat.)* Oh. Apartheid?

DENA.   *That's* it. *That's* the word ...

PETER.   No, my play's about Jews who have assimilated into a gentile society.

DENA.   Wow. Oh. I getcha.

DICK.   The Public Theater did it.

DENA.   Hm.

DICK.   The Public Theater in New York? Joe Papp?

DENA.   Oh, yeah. I know him. Wasn't he at Fox?

DICK.   Joe Papp?

DENA.   Yeah, I think he was. Short guy, right?

DICK.   Yeah ...

DENA.   Yeah, he was at Fox. I'm positive.

DICK.   Joe Papp?

DENA.   Jewish guy, right?

DICK.   Yeah ...

DENA.   I did meet him. At Fox.

PETER.   I really don't think so.

DICK.   *(Over "think so.")* Yeah? Maybe. Whataya know? Yeah,

26

I think you're right. Leave it to Dena. Anyhow.... Let's hear this pitch ... *(All eyes are on Peter.)*

TYNE'S VOICE.   Daddy, Consuelo ate Mrs. Fields.

DICK.   *(Calls.)* Tyne? Daddy's in a meeting, honey.

TYNE'S VOICE.   Daddy, I want a cookie, too. I want *two* cookies.

DICK.   *(Overlap; to others.)* Sorry, my kid.

DENA.   *(Overlap.)* Perfectly all right.

DICK.   *(Calls.)* Tyne? Tyney honey? You can have *one.*

TYNE'S VOICE.   I want macadamia with dark chocolate *and* milk chocolate.

DICK.   No, Tyney. One. Pick one.

TYNE'S VOICE.   I want both. Consuelo had one or two, I'm not sure, and she wasn't supposed to have *any.*

DICK.   *(Calls.)* You can have one chocolate and one —

TYNE'S VOICE.   What kind of chocolate? There's dark chocolate and milk chocolate.

DICK.   *(Overlap; calls.)* Daddy's in a meeting, sweetheart, this isn't a good time for this.

TYNE'S VOICE.   Daddy, it's not fair Consuelo should have.

DICK.   Consuelo *shouldn't've* had, okay?! *(To others.)* These fucking ... *(Calls.)* Take a chocolate chip and an oatmeal raisin and —

TYNE'S VOICE.   I don't like oatmeal.

DICK.   Oatmeal is healthier.

TYNE'S VOICE.   I want one macadamia with dark chocolate ...

DICK.   Tyne ...

TYNE'S VOICE.   ... and one milk chocolate chip.

DICK.   Okay! Now leave Daddy alone! So what do you say? Tyne? What do you say, honey? Tyne? Tyney? *(A beat. To others.)* Anyhow ... *(To Peter.)* Let's hear the pitch.

PETER.   Okay. Um ... *Working Mom ...*

DICK.   *(To Dena.)* Don't you love that title?

DENA.   Oh, yeah, I do.

LAURI.   So do I.

DICK.   I love it. *Working Mom:* it just *says* it.

DENA.   It really does.

DICK. *(To Peter.)* Go head.

PETER. Okay, and I see the opening.... The opening's this sweeping pan of the Statue of Liberty? You know, the camera will sweep around it —

DICK. *(Sort of discreetly.)* Skip it.

PETER. Hm?

DICK. Skip it. Cut to the chase.

DENA. No, I'm with you.

DICK. I want you to hear the story. This stuff, it's trimming.

PETER. I just thought I'd give you a sense of the —

DICK. Don't worry about it. Tell the story. Like you did before. Just tell it.

DENA. Yeah, tell me who she is. I'm dying to know who she is.

PETER. All right. Um ... Dena Flanders —

DENA. *(Laughing.)* — "Flanders?"

PETER. Yeah — was a junior at Atlantic City High when —

DENA. Atlantic City? Where is that again?

PETER. New Jersey.

DENA. Oh, right.

PETER. So, when she was a junior in high school —

DENA. Excuse me. Can I say something?

DICK. Sure. Go head. Feel free. That's what you're here for. Jump right in whenever you like.

DENA. Thanks. I was just wondering ...

DICK. I got some Evian for you. Want some?

DENA. No, thanks. Now: Why does she have to be from New Jersey?

PETER. Well ...

DENA. I mean, like, take *me* for instance.

PETER. Uh huh.

DENA. I'm from Wisconsin.

PETER. Yeah ...

DENA. I mean, couldn't she be from Wisconsin? *(A beat.)*

LAURI. Huh. Interesting.

PETER. But this *character* is *from* New Jersey. Where she's from has a lot to do with who she is.

DICK. I think Peter would have to think about that,

wouldn't you, Peter?

PETER.   Um.... Yeah. I'd have to think about that a lot.

DENA.   You see, let me just say something — do you mind?

PETER.   Not at all.

DENA.   The thing about Wisconsin ... I'm *from* Wisconsin, okay? I grew up there. I *know* it. I *lived* it. I know the *people.* I know what Wisconsin *smells* like. *(She inhales.)*

PETER.   Well, gee, that's interesting, I'll have to —

DENA.   There's something about really really knowing a place.... You know what I mean? You don't have to act. I mean from an acting standpoint. You do not have to *act*, it's there, it's in your skin, it's in your soul, it's *just there.*

DICK.   *(Taking to the idea.)* Uh huh, uh huh. I don't hate that.

PETER.   But the story revolves around —

DICK.   I don't hate that at all. I like it, in fact.

PETER.   Wait, but the story ...

DICK.   The story you can always fix. I do not hate this, there's something to it.

DENA.   *(To Dick.)* You know what I mean?

DICK.   I do. I absolutely do. *(To Lauri.)* You know?

LAURI.   Oh, yeah.

PETER.   Wait a second ...

DICK.   Just go on.

PETER.   But where she's from affects everything a*bout* the story.

DICK.   It's a small fix. A tiny thing, just like that. Believe me, bubbie, it's nothing. Just go on.

PETER.   I don't know ...

DICK.   Go *on*. Don't worry about it. Let *us* worry about it.

PETER.   Well, I had her getting pregnant when she was a junior in high school.

DENA.   Oh, how awful.

PETER.   Hm?

DENA.   Pregnant in high school? Isn't that like setting a really bad role model?

PETER.   Well, no, I mean, realistically ...

DENA.   None of the girls at *my* high school ever would've *dreamed* ...

DICK.   Where'd you go to high school?

DENA.   Holy Trinity in Green Bay? I mean, that is like a completely far-fetched idea where I come from, that a girl would get herself *preg*nant ...

PETER.   Yeah, but this is Atlantic City, New Jersey in the sixties.

DENA.   *(After a beat.)* Not the sixties.

PETER.   Hm?

DENA.   I can't say I was in high school in the sixties. Are you kidding?

PETER.   No?

DENA.   That would put me close to forty.

PETER.   Oh. Yes.

DENA.   I can't play close to forty. Next you'll have me playing mothers. *(Peter looks at Dick. A beat.)*

DICK.   We'll fix it.

DENA.   Something wrong?

PETER.   No. I'm just a little confused. The name of the show, the title of the show, after all, is *Working MOM.*

DENA.   I know. And by the way, did I tell you how much I love that title?

PETER.   Yes. You did.

DENA.   Well, I'm only saying: one kid, all right, I can do that. That's like an accident. Okay, I can accept that. We all make mistakes. But more than one (two or three?), I just can't see it. How many did you give her?

PETER.   Well, three.

DENA.   No. Now that's a stretch. We're talking about the public now, too, Peter. I have fans. They're used to seeing me on *Molly's Marauders.* I mean, that's who they think I am. There's an obligation I have. And this is very very important to me. *(To Lauri.)* You're a woman, you know what I mean.

LAURI.   I do, absolutely.

DENA.   It's very important.

LAURI.   Tell me about it.

DICK.   These are all points for discussion. Let's hear what David has to say first.

PETER.   Hm?

DICK.   Go head.

PETER.   Peter.

DICK.   What?

LAURI.   You said "David," Dick.

DICK.   No, I didn't.

DENA.   Yeah, you did. I heard that, too. *(She laughs, the others join her.)*

DICK.   I did? Jesus, who'm I thinking of? Oh, *I* know: *him*, the schmuck. Never mind. Anyway, let's just hear what the guy has.

DENA.   Yes. Let's. And by the way, I think what you've done so far is just great.

LAURI.   Oh, yes.

DICK.   Didn't I tell you he was something?

PETER.   Anyhow ...

DICK.   He can't take a compliment. Look at him.

PETER.   Well, what I had was: her high school boyfriend marries her because she's pregnant. Paulie Vanzetti his name is, or, that's what I called him. You can call him anything you like, it doesn't matter. Anyway, he never really treated her very well, so finally (this is where the pilot starts), she decides to leave him. She takes her kids — or kid, or whatever — and moves in with her mother, a kind of tart-tongued Olympia Dukakis type and —

DENA.   Oh, I love that! Didn't you love her in *Moonstruck?*

LAURI.   Oh, yes!

DENA.   Now if this could be a kind of *Moonstruck-Fried Green Tomatoes*-fish-out-of-water-*Beverly Hills Cop* kind of thing ...

LAURI.   That's interesting. We were thinking of it more in terms of a *Moonstruck-Working Girl-Parenthoo*d-Tracy Chapman urban grit kind of thing.

DICK.   Just think of her as a female *Rocky.*

LAURI.   Yes!

DENA.   I like that.

DICK.   A female *Rocky.* That's all you have to say. Someone you really root for. What more is there to a good story besides rooting for someone?

DENA. I think so, too. You know? That's it, isn't it? Really really caring. God, that's so true. *(To Peter.)* Please. Continue.

PETER. What's the point? I mean, we seem to be all over the place.

DICK. Uh-oh. Somebody's attitude is showing ... *(Dena and Lauri laugh.)* Look at him. He hates me. *(To Peter.)* Bubbie, you gotta let go. It's the collaborative process. Everybody gets to speak his or her mind, writer or no. It's not New York theater anymore. Now go head. Tell us what happens in the pilot.

PETER. Nothing. She gets a job.

DICK. Peter ...

PETER. Okay, she gets a job working in, you know, a kind of storefront law office (they have them back east) and her boss is this old leftie attorney.

LAURI. A crusty Ed Asner-*Lou Grant*-Jerry Stiller type.

DENA. Hm.

DICK. What.

DENA. Nothing. Well.... What if.... What if.... You know what would be fun? What if she went to beauty school?

PETER. No, I don't see how that fits our idea of —

DICK. Shh.

LAURI. Sort of an urban *Steel Magnolias.*

DENA. Yes! Didn't you just love that movie?

LAURI. Oh, yes.

PETER. But I thought we were going for something gritty and socially relevant.

DICK. Who said?

DENA. Well, this way you'd get to bring in a whole lot of interesting characters. You know, the gay guy, the black manicurist, the fat make-up girl? I mean, this really says something about our culture.

LAURI. You know, maybe we don't need all that backstory at all.

DENA. See, I don't think we do.

LAURI. We can get rid of the kids. We don't need the kids.

PETER. *Working Mom* without kids? Interesting.

DENA. If she's this repressed Catholic woman from Wiscon-

32

sin who comes to L.A. to go to beauty school ...

DICK.   I don't hate that. I don't hate that at all.

DENA.   I mean, wow, think of the possibilities, this repressed person in the middle of L.A. with all these freaks?! Talk about fish-out-of-water!

LAURI.   *(To Dick.)* It's a classic MTM-*Cheers*-*Murphy Brown* ensemble show. We could do three-camera, one-set (the beauty school) —

DICK.   I have no problem with that.

LAURI.   — and we could get it set up at NBC like that.

DENA.   Oh, yes!

DICK.   *(To Peter.)* Maybe you should write some of this down.

PETER.   And maybe *you* should go fuck yourself.

DICK.   Uh-oh. There goes that attitude again.

PETER.   You know, Dick? I'm sitting here thinking, "What am I doing here?, I don't need this." And then I realize, "Well, yeah, I do, I do need this, I need the money." And I think, "That's a lousy reason to subject yourself to something like this." But *then* I think, "Well, tough, you've got to survive; hell, even *Faulk*ner did this, this is what a writer has to do, just take the money and run." Okay, well *then* I ask myself: "Shit, is it really worth the humiliation? Is it really worth feeling so scuzzy? Is it worth this constant burning sensation in my stomach?" And the answer comes back: "Yeah. It is. Just do it and stop caring about it so much. Stop thinking so much." But I *can't* stop thinking. I can't stop thinking how I could get by for two months on what it cost you guys to fly me out here. And I can't stop thinking, What is this "unique voice" shit when you won't even let me finish a sentence? *(He stands and gathers his things.)*

LAURI.   Peter. Please. Sit down. We can still make a go of this.

PETER.   *(A lover's farewell.)* No, Lauri. I'm leaving you. We're through. *(He starts to go.)*

DICK.   Hey. *(Peter stops. A beat.)* It's development, bubbie. *(Peter goes. Pause.)*

DENA.   What just happened?

DICK. *(Shrugs, then.)* Typical New York writer shit. *(Dena and Lauri nod and murmur in agreement.)*

BLACKOUT

ALTERNATE ENDING

LAURI. Peter. Please. Sit down. We can still make a go of this.

PETER. *(A lover's farewell.)* No, Lauri. I'm leaving you. We're through. *(He starts to go.)*

DICK. Hey. *(Peter stops. A beat.)* It's development, bubbie. *(Peter goes. Pause. Calls.)* Jen? Jennifer?

JENNIFER'S VOICE. Yes, Dick?

DICK. Get me Peter's agent. Now, Jen. *(To Lauri.)* I want him. Exclusively. Money's no object. We can't let him get on that plane. *(Dena and Lauri nod and murmur in agreement.)*

BLACKOUT

PROPERTY LIST

Shoulder bag (PETER)
Pitching notes (PETER)
Diet Cokes
Evian water
Macrobiotic lunch (DENA)
Duffle bag (DENA)

L.A.

L.A. was commissioned and first presented by New Writers at the Westside, in New York City, on November 18, 1985. It was directed by Olympia Dukakis. The cast was as follows:

MAN (A) ....John Heard
WOMAN (B) ....Deborah Hedwall

L.A.

A bar in Los Angeles. A man (A) and a woman (B), both in their thirties. She chain smokes. He had been looking at a photo in his wallet when she began talking to him. He sounds vaguely Southern.

B.   Texas?

A.   No.

B.   Not Texas? *(A shakes his head.)* Arkansas?

A.   Arkansas?

B.   *(Laughing.)* No?

A.   No.

B.   Say a little more.

A.   "A little more."

B.   No, say more words, let me hear you talk.

A.   I don't know what to *say* ... *(A beat.)*

B.   Tennessee? *(A beat.)*

A.   *(Puts his wallet in his pocket.)* New Jersey.

B.   What?!

A.   New Jersey, I'm from New Jersey.

B.   New *Jersey*?!

A.   Trenton, New Jersey.

B.   You are *kidding* me.

A.   I was *born* in Yonkers.

B.   You were born in *Yonkers*?!

A.   Uh-huh. My mother was at my grandmother's. Her water, *you* know, that's where it broke.

B.   Isn't that wild? *(A shrugs.)* I mean New Jersey. Who would ever've thought that you were from New Jersey?

A.   This is how I talk.

B.   You don't put it on?

A.   Un-uh.

B.   Not even a little?

A.   I swear. *(Shrugs. Pause.)*

B.   Now me.

A.   What.

B.   Guess where I'm from. Guess.

A.   Florida?

B.   How'd you know? *(A shrugs.)* That is amazing.

A.   I got a good ear —

B.   This is freaky.

A.   — for dialects.

B.   I am freaking. What else do you know about me? *(A shrugs.)* Hm? *(A beat.)*

A.   You smoke too much.

B.   I'm sorry.

A.   That's all right.

B.   *(Putting out her cigarette.)* No, I'm really sorry. I should've asked.

A.   *(Overlap "I should've ...")* Really, it's no problem. I was just saying ... an observation, that's all ...

B.   *(Overlap "that's all ...")* You're right, though. You're right. I *do* smoke too much.

A.   *(Overlap "I do ...")* No, please. Don't put it out on account of me. Smoke. I was just saying, that's all. I was just commenting.

B.   You sure?

A.   I'm sure.

B.   It's not disgusting?

A.   No.

B.   You sure? *(A nods.)* I just want you to know I'm generally more polite than this. I mean, I *do* ask.

A.   You were smoking already. Don't apologize.

B.   The minute you mind you'll tell me?

A.   Yeah.

B.   Promise?

A.   Promise. *(B lights up a new cigarette. Pause.)* Nicholson's from New Jersey, too, you know.

B. Yeah? Oh, yeah.

A. And he doesn't sound it either.

B. No, that's true.

A. Maybe it's something in the water makes us talk like this.

B. *(Overlap "makes us ...")* You do not sound like you come from New Jersey, I'll tell you that.

A. I worked with him.

B. Who?

A. Jack. Nicholson. I did a picture with him.

B. Oh, yeah?

A. *Goin' South.*

B. Don't know it.

A. The one he directed.

B. Uh-huh. Didn't see it.

A. *(Dropping the subject.)* Well, anyway ... *(Pause.)*

B. So, you acted with him? That must've been exciting.

A. The best.

B. I bet.

A. Nicholson, Belushi.

B. Belushi – Belushi?

A. John Belushi, yeah.

B. You knew John Belushi?

A. He was in it, too.

B. Wow. I didn't realize that. What's the name of it again?

A. *Goin' South.* Mary Steenburgen, it was her first picture.

B. Wow. I'll have to rent it.

A. Mary, Danny DeVito ...

B. Wow. All these people.

A. Great people.

B. And you.

A. And me. *(Pause.)* It was a gas.

B. I bet.

A. Boy did we tear up New Mexico.

B. Oh, yeah?

A. Place'll never be the same. Every night, every day, partying all the time. Did a lot of drugs. A *lot* of drugs.

B. You do a lot of drugs?

A. Did.

B.   Not anymore?

A.   Nah. A drink, a couple of drinks ...

B.   You don't do heavy stuff do you?

A.   Then I did. What, it was a six week shoot? It was like six weeks in Disneyland. Stoned all the time. Great stuff. The stuff that was available ... great stuff.

B.   But you're not into it anymore?

A.   Nah. I don't *need* it. You know? Picture was over, I stopped. Just like that. It was good while it lasted. I never did a picture before. I mean, I was straight out of New York City ... a showcase here and there, tending bar, you know, the classic actor story, right?

B.   Perfect.

A.   I mean, I never starved, I paid my rent. Maybe I ate shredded wheat for supper every night, but I never starved. A lot of people, friends of mine?, a lot of people had it worse. I worked. Always doing something. Happy as a clam.

B.   Uh huh.

A.   Didn't *have* anything, didn't *need* anything. I could've gone on like that for years and it would've been okay with me. Honestly.

B.   Uh huh.

A.   Do I seem like an honest guy to you?

B.   Honest?

A.   Do I?

B.   Yeah, I guess.

A.   *(Lost in thought for a beat, back on track.)* So what was I saying?

B.   New York. The big break.

A.   Right. See, I was doing the 982nd showcase of *Hatful of Rain,* and this casting agent's assistant's assistant's lover or something happened to see it. Next thing I knew, got sent up for the Nicholson picture.

B.   Wow. I guess these things *do* happen.

A.   Met with Jack once, twice, a third time. Hit if off like we were old buddies I'm telling you, he's like that.

B.   He *seems* like that.

A.   Got the picture, went to New Mexico. When it was done

everybody said why don't I give L.A. a shot.

B.   Me, too, that's why *I'm* here: giving it a shot.

A.   So I hung out, goofing off mostly. Audition here and there. One day had a callback at Paramount?

B.   Yeah...?

A.   You're gonna like this.

B.   I will?

A.   Very Hollywood.

B.   What.

A.   There she was.

B.   Who?

A.   The most beautiful girl in the world.

B.   Oh.

A.   Holding a clipboard, checking things off.

B.   Uh huh.

A.   A P.A. Like a mirage.

B.   A mirage with a clipboard.

A.   I mean, she was so beautiful, her hair, her face.

B.   Uh huh.

A.   I know it sounds corny, she was like the girl of my dreams. Like if I created a woman, she would've looked just like Sandy. Took one look at her and I was hooked, that was it, I was gone. All I wanted was her.

B.   *(Looking for the waiter.)* I need a refill.

A.   Went up and talked to her?, it was like I'd known her all my life.

B.   I can't believe you knew I was from Florida.

A.   Had her in my head so perfect all my life and there she was. Asked her out? Turned me down, she was seeing some guy. I didn't care. Sent her mailgrams, flower grams, candy grams, balloon grams. Sent her postcards, little notes. I mean, when I look back on it, it was pretty romantic.

B.   Sounds it. It really does.

A.   She finally went out with me?

B.   Yeah...?

A.   Got married three weeks later.

B.   Oh, shit. You're married?

A.   No, listen. See, we got married, then I got this series, like right after.

B.   I recognized you. That's how come I said hello.

A.   *(Overlap "... I said ...")* Uh huh. So, I was on a roll. All of a sudden I was making all this money. I mean, I went from unemployment to you know how much I was making?

B.   How much?

A.   Guess.

B.   I don't know.

A.   I'll tell you, not because I'm bragging or anything. I don't brag. I'm not a bragger.

B.   No.

A.   I'll tell you, only 'cause I can hardly believe it myself.

B.   How *much?*

A.   In two years on this series?

B.   Yeah...?

A.   And it was just a small little role really.

B.   How *much?!*

A.   Made close to four hundred grand.

B.   What?!

A.   Four hundred thousand dollars.

B.   That's unbelievable.

A.   Before taxes.

B.   That's still unbelievable.

A.   And take out for my agent.

B.   Still.

A.   That's gross.

B.   So much money!

A.   I know. It's embarrassing almost.

B.   Why should you be embarrassed?

A.   I don't know. That's for doing a stupid little role week after week. It doesn't seem right.

B.   Oh, the hell with it.

A.   We're talking about a nothing series. I know what it is, I don't kid myself. I mean, some of these people doing some of the worst garbage, you should hear them, it's like they're doing *Hamlet* or something.

B.   I would love to get even a little tiny part. I don't kid myself either. The whole medium ...

A. I mean my series, it's *okay.*

B. Uh huh.

A. It's not like something I'm really really proud of.

B. Of course not. It's a living.

A. Yeah, but who needs all that money. I'm an actor.

B. Hey, I'm dying to get *anything.* You're very lucky.

A. I am lucky.

B. You're very lucky.

A. I don't mean to complain.

B. I know.

A. I'm just commenting. This is the situation. There are too many rich people out here.

B. In the medium?

A. In the medium, in the field. Too much money, too many *things.* It's no good.

B. Ultimately, you mean.

A. Yeah. I mean, you should drive around Bel Air.

B. I have!

A. You should see how these people live.

B. I know!

A. I mean, I like money, sure. I love money. I want nice things.

B. So do *I.*

A. I mean we *all* want nice things.

B. *I* do.

A. The American Dream and everything.

B. The American Dream, that's *right* ...

A. It's true.

B. Oh I know.

A. There's truth in The American Dream.

B. You're looking at another sucker who bought it.

A. I mean it's real.

B. Very real, yes. We all want things, we all aspire.

A. Yes.

B. Why do you think I came to Hollywood.

A. The same thing.

B. To seek fame and fortune.

A. We work and we want to be rewarded.

B. We feel we *deserve.*

A. That's right. We all want to live nice and give our kids whatever we can possibly give them. My little girl ...

B. You have a little girl? I didn't know you had a little girl.

A. *(Takes out wallet.)* Almost two.

B. Oh, my God, she's so beautiful.

A. Next month she'll be two. That right? Yeah, the 28th.

B. She is darling.

A. Katie her name is.

B. Katie.

A. I love this kid. She cracks me up.

B. Yeah? Wait, I'm not done. *(Meaning with the picture.)*

A. I am so crazy about her. I got her more toys ...

B. I bet.

A. Her room is like a toy store. And she's so small. You can't find her. See, I'm the kind of father, I see something makes me think of her, I buy it. Not just dolls and stuff. Posters, paintings. Things I think she'll appreciate when she's older. I can't help it. I'm always buying her things.

B. That's nice.

A. I don't know, I try to stop but I can't.

B. You're always thinking of her.

A. Yeah, but maybe enough is enough. I bought her a pony.

B. Wow.

A. I think maybe I shouldn't've. My wife's allergic, so she can't take care of it. And Katie's too small. So I had to hire someone. That adds up after a while.

B. I love horses.

A. Whoever invented credit cards ... I mean, I see something, I whip out the plastic and I don't even think twice. I love buying presents.

B. You're a generous person.

A. I don't know, think maybe I go overboard. I know I do.

B. Not necessarily.

A. I do. I see something I like, I want it, I got to have it. My wife and I.... You ever been to Beverly Hills?

B. Sure.

A. Well, I just *had* to live in Beverly Hills. Don't know why,

I got this idea in my head I'm a successful TV star now and I got to live in Beverly Hills.

B.   The American Dream thing.

A.   That's right.

B.   You *deserve* to live in Beverly Hills.

A.   I guess. Well, so, I got the most beautiful house. One look, I knew I had to have it. A real house. My first real house. Four bedrooms, pool, garden. I love that house. But not only do you buy the house, but you got to pay for the gardener, and the housekeeper, and the babysitter, and the insurance, and then you need a couple of cars ... I got her this custom pink Mercedes for our anniversary. Had a fit but she loves it. I mean, I kind of went on this spree. Thought what the hell, it's only money. I mean I went nuts. I love gadgets. VCRs, microwaves, big-screen TVs, state-of-the-art stereo, state-of-the-art burglar alarm. It was fun in the beginning. We used to joke about it. I was like a guy at the craps table. Or a coke fiend or something. I mean, some people blow their dough on dope. Not me, that doesn't interest me. If I want to get stoned, I got friends I can visit. You know what I mean?

B.   Uh huh.

A.   I got friends for that. That's not my idea of what I want out of life. I like things that *last*. Not something that lasts as long as a high. I mean cameras, a synthesizer because I want to get back into music.

B.   You're into music? I sing!

A.   Truth is, this computer I bought, it's still in the *box*. Got it almost a year ago. See, I went too far and I know it. Went completely overboard. My credit stopped. One day, just like that, like the well was dry.

B.   Hm.

A.   My wife threw me out.

B.   Oh, no.

A.   Oh, this is a while ago. Really woke me up, I tell you. A real slap in the face. I mean when something like that happens you stop and say to yourself, "Whoa, hey, man, you're going over the deep end." Really opened my eyes.

B.   Uh huh.

A.   I told her, "Honey, you really opened my eyes. I'll change. I understand my problem now."

B.   Uh huh.

A.   Divorced me anyhow.

B.   Oh ...

A.   You know how much a divorce costs?

B.   I can imagine.

A.   I'm not even gonna tell you 'cause it would make you sick and I don't want you losing all that good alcohol. A lot of money. A *lot* of money. Lawyers and lawyers and more lawyers. You ever deal with a lawyer?

B.   Legally? No.

A.   Assholes. One asshole's bigger than the one before. Don't ever need a lawyer. What a system. Designed to destroy people.

B.   What.

A.   How divorce works. They want to destroy me. Did I tell you my series got cancelled today?

B.   Oh, no, you didn't.

A.   I'm not worried. I always got *some*thing. What did I need all that money for anyway? All I've got now is this little studio. A bed, a TV.

B.   Back to basics, right?

A.   Yeah. Took it so I could be near my daughter. I see her every day. My wife's cool about that, thank God. She knows I'm not gonna run away with her or anything. Though, I tell you, I've thought about it. I have thought about it.

B.   I don't know about that. That gives me the creeps.

A.   I'm an honest guy ... I don't know, sometimes I think if I really want something.... She's crazy about me, my little girl. *(Pause.)* I tell ya, when I was knocking around New York ...

B.   Uh huh.

A.   Working here and there ...

B.   Yeah...?

A.   I had this secret fantasy.

B.   Tell me yours and I'll tell you mine.

A.   I had this fantasy that one day I was gonna make it, not

48

big, big enough, you know, a steady income coming in ...

B.   Uh huh.

A.   And I'd treat my friends who weren't working to a good dinner every now and then, and help 'em get work, and fall in love and get married for life, for *life*, and have a couple of kids, and give those kids everything I could give them, and live in style, not showy, but in style, and that was all I wanted. That was my secret fantasy. That's not a bad fantasy, right? *(B shakes her head; pauses; looks at the photo in his wallet, then puts it away; pause.)* So what's yours. *(As she opens her mouth to speak.)*

BLACKOUT

PROPERTY LIST

Wallet (A) with:
    photograph
Cigarettes (B)
Cigarette lighter or matches (B)
Glasses

SPACE

SPACE was commissioned and first presented by New Writers at the Westside, in New York City, in June, 1986. It was directed by Chris Silva. The cast was as follows:

MAN (A) ....Dennis Boutsikaris
MAN (B) ....John Griesemer

SPACE

Two men, A and B, in their mid-thirties. Late at night, after eating, drinking, and smoking dope. B's apartment.

A. *(Speaks very slowly.)* You're out there. In the middle of the desert. At night. And you turn off the headlights. And you're. The darkness. Like you're floating. In space. Like you're in space. You *feel* it. You *feel*. The nothingness. The, the. The *huge*ness. The utter. Vastness. Of space. And you'd think it should be quiet. Because it's so black. Because of all the nothingness. But, no. Then your ears. The motor is off. You turn off the motor and you hear. This buzz. This, this *symphony*. Of life. Of living things, you know? *(Pause.)*

B. We never went to the desert, me and Nan.

A. Oh, it's elemental. It's. There's so much life like you're not even aware of out there. All that emptiness. All that seemingly empty space. *(Pause.)*

B. I *wanted* to. She wasn't interested.

A. 'Cause the thing is. What makes it so elemental, the desert. Are the contradictions. You know what I mean?

B. Uh huh.

A. The contradictions. Like the temperature. You're sweaty *and* cold. At the same time. What do you call it?

B. What.

A. At the same time.

B. Simultaneously?

A. Yes, but that's not the word.

B. Um ...

A. That's not what I'm thinking of. *(Pause.)*

B. Concurrently?

A. No ...

B. Happening at the same time?

53

A.   I can't think.

B.   Anyway ...

A.   Anyway, the temperature. Paradoxes? Do I mean paradoxes?

B.   Paradoxes?, yes.

A.   Maybe. Maybe that's what I mean. Something and yet something else?, something that seemingly. Contradicts. The first thing?

B.   Yeah ...

A.   Days. It could go above. The temperature could *surpass* a hundred, hundred and *ten* sometimes. At night. The temperature. Could drop sixty degrees easy. Plummet. The temperature plummets. The mercury. Way down.

B.   I should've just taken off and gone by myself.

A.   Wait: so, you're out there. In all this space. And this buzzing?

B.   *(Preoccupied, then testily.)* What?

A.   *(After a beat.)* Are you mad at me or something?

B.   No.

A.   I'm painting a picture for you. What it was like.

B.   Go ahead.

A.   *(After a beat, meaning, "What's the matter?")* What.

B.   Nothing. Tell me. Paint.

A.   *(After a beat, proceeding cautiously.)* There's this buzzing. This music. I mean it. It *is* like a symphony or something. These creatures. Crickets and insects. And. Creatures. Sounds. Coming. Emanating. Coming out of the air, almost. Yeah, it seems to come out of the air. Or up through the earth. Like the sand is, is. The earth's skin. And this sound. This electricity. Yeah, it's an *electrical* sound. This sound seeps out of the earth's pores. And you feel yourself hum with it. You feel the buzz of your own aura. Like your lifeforce has a sound, too. Just like the lizards and the crickets and the creatures and stuff. You know?

B.   Yeah ...

A.   And the next thing that happens. The next thing you're *aware* of. And the thing is, we weren't even stoned yet. That's right, we weren't. On purpose. We wanted to be straight. At least in the beginning. So we could experience it, you know, unadulterated. So we could come to our own conclusions, you know?

B. Uh huh.

A. Without drugs.

B. That's good.

A. You know? With*out* drugs. *Later* we got stoned. But in the beginning ...

B. You were straight.

A. We were straight. That was a choice. A conscious decision. And I'm glad.

B. Uh huh?

A. I'm very glad. *(A beat.)* So what was I saying? *(Pause.)*

B. The —

A. Oh! So, the next thing you notice. After the buzz. Your eyes. They adjust to the darkness. And you know what?

B. What?

A. It isn't dark at all. It's like almost blindingly lit up. The desert is. Illuminated. By the moon! I'm talking just like seconds into it. Once you adjust. A) the buzz. B) the brightness. You can see everything in sight! Mountains and bushes and cactuses. Cacti. And like lizards 'tween your toes. And clouds! You can see a couple of clouds! And the moon! It's true! The moon is like a silver hole in the sky lighting up everything in sight! And stars twinkle like they're special effects or something. It's unreal. It is unreal. And we take off our clothes. It's like me and Katie, we're Adam and Eve. And the desert is our garden. And then we did it.

B. Uh huh.

A. Unbelievable.

B. I bet.

A. No, the feeling. This feeling of, of. Of nature. Of being a part of the cosmic buzz, you know? God. Amazing. *(Pause. Sadly.)* We had such a great time out west. *(Pause.)*

B. You want to sleep on the couch?

A. No, no.

B. It's no hassle. You *can.*

A. No, I'll go. I'll go home.

B.   'Cause I have to get up early.

A.   I understand.

B.   I'm temping

A.   I understand.

B.   I've got to shlep all the way out to Long Island City.

A.   I understand, really.

B.   Some *furni*ture place.

A.   I'll get out of your way.

B.   'Cause you're welcome to ...

A.   *(Not budging.)* I'll go home.

B.   I mean it. *(A nods, "I know." Pause.)* Well, here we are. *(A beat.)* Did you ever think we'd end up like this, you and me? *(A shakes his head.)* Me neither. I thought I'd've been a father by now. Nan was making good money, we could've had a kid.

A.   What is it with these women? *(B continues shaking his head. After a beat.)* I don't understand it. This trip out west. Things were never better.

B.   I know, pal.

A.   Everything had seemed to come together. But. At the same time. Everything was falling apart.

B.   I know.

A.   It's a paradox.

B.   I'm really sorry. I really am.

A.   Let's analyze this. *(B's heart sinks.)* I felt we were never closer. *She* felt closed-in. That's what she told me. We were watching the sun rise and it's like she went cold on me. Like she shut off the juice.

B.   You're gonna drive yourself nuts, you know that?

A.   I should've known. I should've seen it coming. *(He smacks his own forehead.)*

B.   Hey!

A.   *(After a beat.)* We were. You know. While we were doing it? Katie was on top. Bouncing. Her hair blowing in the stars. Both of us breathing hard. Buzzing along with everything else. Sand crunching my back. The sweat and the goosebumps. Everything, in other words. Everything. I was watching Katie go. Bouncing. Her eyes closed. I was watching Katie. And over by her ear. In the sky. I saw it. We went to the desert to see Halley's comet. And there it was. Katie wearing it like an earring. I didn't tell her. I didn't want to ruin it. Halley's comet. I'm sure it was. This smudge. This nothing little white smudge. Halley's comet. *(He shakes his head in disappointment. A beat.)*

B.   I'm getting you a pillow. You're sleeping on the couch. *(He goes. A continues to shake his head.)*

BLACKOUT

WOMEN
IN MOTION

WOMEN IN MOTION was commissioned and first presented by the Lucille Ball Festival for New Comedy (David Munnell, Artistic Director), in Jamestown, New York, on May 24, 1991. It was directed by Rand Foerster. The cast was as follows:

LIBBY .... Kathryn Rossetter
MONICA .... Carol McCann

CHARACTERS

LIBBY and MONICA, two single women in their 30s, who are vacationing together.

SCENES

1. On a Plane
2. At Poolside
3. In the Hotel Bar
4. Outside Their Hotel Room
5. On a Plane

WOMEN IN MOTION

SCENE 1

On a Plane

The Women have been drinking. Spirits are high. A friendly argument is in progress.

LIBBY.   But she's a prostitute!

MONICA.   She's not a prostitute, she's, *you* know, a *call* girl.

LIBBY.   That's not a call girl, Monica, a call girl doesn't hang out on Sunset Boulevard. That's a hooker. She's a hooker.

MONICA.   But she's not *into* it. She's *new* at it.

LIBBY.   He doesn't know that. Why would a guy who looked like that have to pick up a hooker in the first place?

MONICA.   He was lost, remember?

LIBBY.   Bullshit.

MONICA.   He *was*. Don't you remember? That's why she got in with him.

LIBBY.   Give me a break. A guy who looks like that, with the kind of money he had, he could have *any*body, why would he want a hooker from the streets?

MONICA.   Because she was beautiful.

LIBBY.   Uch, did you think she was beautiful?

MONICA.   Yes!

LIBBY.   With that awful wig? She wasn't beautiful.

MONICA.   But that's the thing: he could *tell* that she was really beautiful.

LIBBY. Not when he picked her up in the car he couldn't. How could he? The girl she was *with* was more attractive.

MONICA. Did you think so? Uch, I didn't think so at all.

LIBBY. It didn't make any sense to me why he would go for *her*.

MONICA. God, Libby, where's your imagination? Where's your sense of romance?

LIBBY. I don't see what's so romantic about picking up a prostitute who could give you AIDS, and letting her live in your hotel room with you.

MONICA. Libby ...

LIBBY. How did *he* know she wasn't a drug addict or something?

MONICA. What?!

LIBBY. She could've ripped him off or killed him or something.

MONICA. God, Libby, it's a *movie*, it's not real life.

LIBBY. I *know* it's a movie, Monica.

MONICA. Of *course* in real life you'd have to ask questions, but it's a *movie*.

LIBBY. I can't believe you saw it so many times. *How* many times did you see it?

MONICA. I don't even know anymore. I bought the tape for 14.99? I leave it in my VCR. Every night I watch a little bit before I go to sleep.

LIBBY. I don't be*lieve* you! *Every* night?

MONICA. So? Don't you look at a book sometimes before you go to sleep?

LIBBY. Yeah, but not the same book every night.

MONICA. It helps me fall asleep, okay? I *love* this movie. I can't believe you didn't love it.

LIBBY. Don't take it so personal; we're gonna be together the next five nights and six days, you shouldn't take it so personal.

MONICA. I'm not. *(A beat.)* I'm sorry you didn't like it.

LIBBY. It's only a movie, you know ...

MONICA. I know.

LIBBY.   ... it's not the end of the world.

MONICA.   I know. *(A beat.)* Maybe 'cause you saw it on a plane.

LIBBY.   Monica, I wouldn't't've liked it even if I saw it Radio City.

MONICA.   How could you tell if you liked something on a plane? You can't tell on a plane, these plastic things sticking in your ears, people keeping their shades up. Besides, they cut the best scene. The best scene she goes down on him, he's watching Lucy.

LIBBY.   Which one?

MONICA.   Which what?

LIBBY.   Which Lucy?

MONICA.   The one with the grapes.

LIBBY.   Oh, yeah. *(She smiles.)*

MONICA.   Next time you come over, I'll play it.

LIBBY.   I don't *want* to see it again.

MONICA.   I'll play you the *scene* I'm talking about. It's a sexy scene. Don't you think he's sexy? *(Libby shrugs.)* You *don't?* I can't believe you don't think he's sexy.

LIBBY.   He's all right.

MONICA.   All *right?* He's gorgeous.

LIBBY.   He doesn't do it for me, Monica, what can I tell ya.

MONICA.   Don't you think he's aged like really incredibly well?

LIBBY.   That I agree with. I never liked his looks. He always looked so smoothed out, you know, like his face had something missing.

MONICA.   Don't you think he looks a little like Mike?

LIBBY.   Like *Mike?* Are you kidding?

MONICA.   No?

LIBBY.   He looks nothing like Mike.

MONICA.   How can you say that? Mike is gorgeous.

LIBBY.   Mike is very good *look*ing but he's not gorgeous, I wouldn't call Mike gorgeous. You always had this thing for Mike. I don't get it.

MONICA.   Oh, God, when he gets close to me to give me something to type? I feel like my heart is making so much noise he can hear me and I get embarrassed. I love the way he smells. Aramis he wears.

LIBBY. How do you know?

MONICA. My brother wears it. *(A beat.)* What's his story do you think?

LIBBY. Mike?

MONICA. Yeah. You don't think he's *gay* or anything.

LIBBY. *Mike?* No.

MONICA. I mean, any man that dresses that good ...

LIBBY. Mike is not gay.

MONICA. You sure?

LIBBY. I'm sure. Believe me, I'm sure.

MONICA. Uh huh. *(A beat.)* What's that mean?

LIBBY. What's what.

MONICA. What you just said. The way you said it, what do you mean?

LIBBY. Nothing.

MONICA. You said it like you know something.

LIBBY. Monica, will you stop analyzing everything I say and do?

MONICA. *Tell* me. How do *you* know so much about Mike? You've been in the office less than I have.

LIBBY. I don't know, I just know.

MONICA. Libby ...

LIBBY. *(A beat.)* He came on to me, okay.

MONICA. You're kidding me.

LIBBY. No.

MONICA. When?

LIBBY. Before the Christmas party.

MONICA. Be*fore?* Where?

LIBBY. By the Xerox.

MONICA. You're kidding me.

LIBBY. Un-uh.

MONICA. You were in the Xerox room with Mike?

LIBBY. Uh huh.

MONICA. What were you doing?

LIBBY. Xeroxing.

MONICA. And he came in?

LIBBY. Uh huh.

MONICA. Just the two of you?

LIBBY. Yeah. Well, Carmen was there, too. She was collating but she left.

MONICA. So it was just you and Mike?

LIBBY. Uh huh.

MONICA. I'm dying. I can't believe you didn't tell me this.

LIBBY. I didn't want to upset you. I know you have this thing for Mike.

MONICA. You're right, you were smart, it's a good thing. So what happened?

LIBBY. The Xerox started eating paper.

MONICA. Yeah? So what you do?

LIBBY. We fixed it.

MONICA. You and Mike?

LIBBY. Uh huh.

MONICA. Together?

LIBBY. Yeah. You know, I pulled out the thing, he pulled out the paper.

MONICA. And?

LIBBY. And he asked me what I was doing for vacation.

MONICA. He did? So what you tell him?

LIBBY. I told him I was going the Caribbean with *you.*

MONICA. Oh, God, you told him you were going with *me?*

LIBBY. Christ, Monica, calm down.

MONICA. I'm sorry. So what he say?

LIBBY. He said, "Oh, that's nice."

MONICA. He did?

LIBBY. Something like that. And then he asked me what I was doing New Year's.

MONICA. You're kidding me.

LIBBY. No.

MONICA. Mike asked *you* what you were doing New Year's? You mean Mike isn't seeing anyone? Don't you think if he asked you what you were doing New Year's that means he was free?

LIBBY. I don't know, maybe he just wanted to know.

MONICA. Why would he want to know something like that?

LIBBY. Maybe he was just curious, I don't know. Do you want me to tell you this or not?

MONICA. Yes yes yes, I'm sorry. So anyway go on. He asked you what you were doing New Year's and ...

LIBBY. I said we were flying home on the first.

MONICA. Yeah...?

LIBBY. And he said, "That's too bad." He and Ed McCarthy are throwing a party.

MONICA. Oh. Ed McCarthy from Accounting?

LIBBY. I guess.

MONICA. How come *I* didn't know about this party?

LIBBY. I don't know, I didn't either.

MONICA. Yeah, but he told *you*. He practically in*vited* you.

LIBBY. But I couldn't go. I was going here with you.

MONICA. Yeah, but nobody told *me*. How come nobody invited *me?*

LIBBY. Monica, everybody knew you were going away. Nobody invited me either. 'Cause they knew you and me were going the Caribbean. I knew I shouldn't've told you.

MONICA. I'm not upset. I'm not. This is very interesting. How come nobody told me about this party.

LIBBY. I don't understand you. We're on our way the Caribbean. What do *you* care about this stupid party?

MONICA. I don't. I'm only saying isn't this interesting. *(Libby looks through a magazine. Pause.)* I'm *glad* we're not gonna be there, aren't you?

LIBBY. It doesn't matter to me one way or the other, Monica, I don't care about the stupid party.

MONICA. I know, you're right. *(Pause.)* Uh! I can't wait till we're sitting in the sun, right?

LIBBY. I know. Me, neither.

MONICA. I cannot wait. *(Pause.)*

LIBBY. Please, God, let there be sex.

MONICA. Amen. *(They laugh.)*

End of Scene

SCENE 2

At Poolside

The Women, in bathing suits, on chaise lounge chairs. Monica is reading a romance novel. Libby, lying on her stomach with her bikini straps undone, is reading a magazine.

MONICA. Can you believe this place?

LIBBY. Mm.

MONICA. It's gorgeous. It's like paradise. Looks just like the brochure. Doesn't it?

LIBBY. Yeah.

MONICA. Not a cloud in the sky, the water.... Can you believe that water? This place is totally unreal. When I saw the water in the brochure I thought: Can't be, there *is* no such color, they made up a color like that. But can you believe that color?

LIBBY. Mm. I know. *(Pause.)*

MONICA. I'm *so* glad we did this. Aren't you?

LIBBY. Oh, yeah.

MONICA. Uch, can you imagine being in the city?

LIBBY. Yeah.

MONICA. The crowds and the cold and everything? Uch, if I had to spend another Christmas with my family ... *(Pause.)* I can't believe we just got here. I was just thinking to myself, isn't this funny? I feel like we've been here for days. Don't you? Don't you feel like you've been here for days?

LIBBY. Mm.

MONICA. I feel like we've been here a week. I feel so relaxed. I can't believe how relaxed I feel. *(A beat.)* You should put some stuff on, you know. You're burning.

LIBBY. I am?

MONICA. You want me to?

LIBBY. I *put* some stuff on. I put 25.

MONICA.   I know but you're burning anyway. I can tell with these sunglasses. You're turning pink. Your shoulders. They say if you sweat or swim.... You want me to do it?

LIBBY.   You mind?

MONICA.   Not at all.

LIBBY.   Thanks, it's in my thing. *(Monica gets a bottle of sun block out of Libby's bag and applies the lotion.)*

MONICA.   You have pretty skin.

LIBBY.   Thank you.

MONICA.   My back breaks out. *(A beat.)* Wasn't lunch great?

LIBBY.   It was all right.

MONICA.   Just all right? Didn't you think it was delicious?

LIBBY.   It was chicken salad with pineapple in it.

MONICA.   Yeah, I know, I thought it was delicious. What an interesting combination. I'm gonna have to try that. Tropical chicken salad.

LIBBY.   It was canned pineapple.

MONICA.   That wasn't canned pineapple.

LIBBY.   Yes it was. It was a ring. Like you get from Dole.

MONICA.   Libby, that was not canned pineapple. This is the tropics. They *grow* pineapple here. What do they need to get it from cans for?

LIBBY.   I'm telling you, mine had a piece of ring in it. Fresh pineapple doesn't come in rings, that much I know.

MONICA.   So what if it was?

LIBBY.   Was what?

MONICA.   So what if it did come from a can? Does that mean it wasn't good?

LIBBY.   All I'm saying, for what they charge you, they could at least give you fresh pineapple. That's all I'm saying. *(Pause.)*

MONICA.   *(Quietly.)* I thought it was very good. *(A beat.)* I suppose you didn't like the dessert either?

LIBBY.   No, the dessert was good.

MONICA.   Oh. Well. *(Libby ties her bikini top and sits up.)*

LIBBY.   Monica. Why must you take everything so personal?

MONICA.   I don't.

LIBBY.   Yes, you do. I tell you it was canned pineapple and you get all huffy with me.

MONICA. I do not get huffy.

LIBBY. Okay. Whatever you say. *(Pause.)*

MONICA. I'm sorry you didn't like the chicken salad.

LIBBY. I said it was all right! I didn't say I didn't like it! It's not like you *made* it!

MONICA. I know.

LIBBY. It's really no big deal!

MONICA. Okay! *(Long pause. Both resume reading.)* We're not having a fight, are we.

LIBBY. Who said we're having a fight?

MONICA. I'm only asking.

LIBBY. No we are not having a fight.

MONICA. Good. I didn't think so. *(Pause.)* I hate fights.

LIBBY. This isn't a fight.

MONICA. I know, I'm just saying. My parents used to fight all the time. It was horrible. The stupidest things they'd fight about. *(A beat.)* Can we go dancing tonight please?

End of Scene

SCENE 3

In the Bar of the Hotel

The Women are seated at a table drinking daiquiris and watching other people dance. Music.

LIBBY. Wait, look at *her.*

MONICA. Who.

LIBBY. The one with the hair.

MONICA. Oh, God! *Look* at her! She looks like Ann-Margret or something. Can you believe men actually find that attractive?

LIBBY. *He* does.

MONICA. You think he's her husband?

LIBBY. No way, are you kidding?, they probably just met

down here.

MONICA.   Uch. Really? Look how she's letting him hold her.

LIBBY.   I know.

MONICA.   His hands are all over her.

LIBBY.   Some guys get off on that. Public display.

MONICA.   I think it's digusting.

LIBBY.   They probably already did it.

MONICA.   You think?

LIBBY.   Why not?

MONICA.   I don't know. They're not even tan.

LIBBY.   So?

MONICA.   I mean, if they're not tan, they couldn't've been down here very long; how long could they have known each other?

LIBBY.   Unless ...

MONICA.   What.

LIBBY.   Unless they're in their room *doing* it all the time.

MONICA.   Uch. You think?

LIBBY.   He *is* holding her awfully familiar.

MONICA.   I know; he is. I just can't believe people do it so quickly anymore.

LIBBY.   You were in the ladies' room.

MONICA.   So?

LIBBY.   When was the last time you saw a condom machine in a ladies' room?

MONICA.   I never noticed.

LIBBY.   Oh, come on.

MONICA.   No, really, I never noticed. I thought people weren't having sex anymore.

LIBBY.   No, people *are* having sex; you and *I* aren't having sex anymore. *(A beat.) That's* an attractive couple.

MONICA.   Where?

LIBBY.   The Kevin Costner-looking guy in white and the woman with quite a butt.

MONICA.   Oh, yeah, they are. You think they're on their honeymoon or something?

LIBBY.   Maybe.

MONICA.   They do look good together, don't they. *(Libby nods. They watch the couple for a long beat.)* How old do you think they are? Younger than us?

LIBBY.   I hate to say it.

MONICA.   I think so, too.

LIBBY.   I like *him.*

MONICA.   That's 'cause he looks so happily married.

LIBBY.   That's right. Uh-oh, don't look now.

MONICA.   What.

LIBBY.   We're being scoped.

MONICA.   You're kidding.

LIBBY.   The guys with the glasses diagonally across.

MONICA.   Oh, my God, you're right.

LIBBY.   Staring straight at us.

MONICA.   Can you believe that? I thought that went out in the high school cafeteria.

LIBBY.   Got our attention, didn't it.

MONICA.   What should we do?

LIBBY.   Does either of them interest you in any way?

MONICA.   I don't know. I can't tell. They look alike.

LIBBY.   I know. *(A beat.)* Do we want to pursue this?

MONICA.   I don't know, do we? I mean, hell, we *are* on vacation.

LIBBY.   What is that supposed to mean?

MONICA.   I mean, I want to dance. We're supposed to be enjoying ourselves.

LIBBY.   Do those guys look like we'd enjoy ourselves? *(They look at them for a moment.)*

MONICA.   Good question.

LIBBY.   Do they?

MONICA.   Well, the one with the high forehead?

LIBBY.   Yeah?

MONICA.   Looks like he might have a nice smile.

LIBBY.   It's not his *smile* I'm interested in, Monica. *(They giggle like schoolgirls.)* Uh-oh.

MONICA.   What.

LIBBY. They're coming over.
MONICA. Oh, shit.

End of Scene

SCENE 4

Outside Their Hotel Room

Later that night. A "Do not disturb" sign hangs from the doorknob. Libby is beside herself. She paces, looks at her watch, knocks at the door several times.

LIBBY. Monica? Monica, open the door. Come on. *(A beat. Another knock.)* Monica? Please don't make me use my key and walk in on you. I know you're in there. I have my key, Monica, don't make me use it. That would really be gross. *(A beat. Another knock.)* Monica, open up, it's quarter to four, please, I want to go to bed. The deal was three. I gave you an extra forty-five minutes, please, Monica. *(Monica, wrapped in a sheet, opens the door.)*
MONICA. Shh. Steve is sleeping.
LIBBY. I don't *care* Steve is sleeping, wake him up.
MONICA. I can't just wake him up.
LIBBY. Why not? God, Monica, it's almost four o'clock in the morning —
MONICA. Shhh.
LIBBY. — and I want to go to sleep in my own bed in my own hotel room that I paid half of!
MONICA. What happened to Bruce?
LIBBY. Bruce was an asshole.
MONICA. Why?
LIBBY. Please would you just wake him up.
MONICA. What happened?
LIBBY. Nothing happened. Would you please just hand him his pants?

MONICA.   Are you okay?

LIBBY.   No I'm not okay. I'm tired. I want to go to sleep.

MONICA.   When you didn't come at three, I figured you were staying in *their* room.

LIBBY.   Why would I stay in their room?

MONICA.   I don't know.

LIBBY.   You thought I was gonna *sleep* with that asshole?

MONICA.   I thought he seemed nice.

LIBBY.   God, Monica.

MONICA.   I thought you two looked like you really hit it off.

LIBBY.   What's your definition of really hitting it off? What, 'cause I didn't throw up?

MONICA.   Libby ... *(A beat.)* I'm really sorry you didn't have a nice time.

LIBBY.   Will you stop taking everything so personal?! You don't have to tell me you're sorry!

MONICA.   That's not what I mean. I mean I *did* have a nice time. I'm *having* a nice time. Steve is very nice. *(Pause.)* Really, Libby, when you didn't come to the room at three, Steve and I, we just assumed.

LIBBY.   What did you and Steve assume.

MONICA.   *You* know. That you and Bruce. That you were having as nice a time as we were having.

LIBBY.   *(A beat.)* Bruce left around twelve thirty.

MONICA.   You're kidding, he left you in the bar?

LIBBY.   Uh huh.

MONICA.   Why?

LIBBY.   I didn't want to sleep with him. I told him if he thought he was gonna get me in bed that he might as well give up now and go to sleep or try to pick somebody else up.

MONICA.   And?

LIBBY.   And he thanked me for my honesty and said good night.

MONICA.   Uch, you're kidding me.

LIBBY.   No.

MONICA.   So you've been sitting in the bar all this time?

LIBBY.   I had to come up. They were washing the floor.

MONICA.   Oh, God, I'm sorry. I mean, *you* know. *(A beat.)*
Hey, tomorrow Steve and I are gonna go snorkeling. You want
to come?
LIBBY.   *(A beat.)* No, thanks.
MONICA.   You sure?
LIBBY.   Positive.
MONICA.   'Cause I'm sure he wouldn't mind.
LIBBY.   Gee, that's very thoughtful of you.
MONICA.   *(A beat.)* You mean it?
LIBBY.   What do *you* think? *(Long pause.) Look* at you.
MONICA.   What.
LIBBY.   With your sheet and everything. You look like Julia
Roberts or something.
MONICA.   Yeah? *(Pause.)*
LIBBY.   So, are you gonna wake him up or what?
MONICA.   I guess. *(Pause. She stays put.)*
LIBBY.   Well? *(Pause. Monica reluctantly turns to reenter the
room.)* Monica?
MONICA.   Yeah?
LIBBY.   Something I didn't tell you me and Mike in the
Xerox room.
MONICA.   *(A beat.)* Yeah...? *(Pause.)*
LIBBY.   He kissed me. With his tongue and everything. *(Long
pause. Monica returns to the room, closing the door behind her.)*

End of Scene

SCENE 5

On a Plane

Libby is wearing headphones and looking out the window. Monica is applying polish to her nails.

AIRPLANE PILOT'S VOICE.   Ladies and gentlemen, we're still circling over the New York area awaiting clearance to land. We're next in line, though, so we should be on the ground in, oh I'd say, eight to ten minutes. Sorry for the inconvenience, folks. At this time, on behalf of the flight crew and myself, I'd like to thank you for flying United, and wish you a happy and a healthy new year. We'd also like to wish you good luck in the New York City area, or whatever your final destination might be. *(The Women do not speak.)*

END OF PLAY

PROPERTY LIST

Magazine (LIBBY)
Romance novel (MONICA)
Pool bag (LIBBY) with:
    sunblock lotion bottle
"Do not disturb" sign for doorknob
Watch (LIBBY)
Headphones (LIBBY)
Nail polish (MONICA)

ZIMMER

A Play in One Act for One Actor

ZIMMER was commissioned and first presented by the Jewish Repertory Theater (Ran Avni, Artistic Director; Edward M. Cohen, Artistic Associate), in New York City, on February 24, 1987. It was directed by Michael Arabian and performed by Joe Urla.

AUTHOR'S NOTE

The actor portraying the many characters depicted in this play should not resort to caricature, but instead capture the essence of the various men and women. The rapid transitions should have the effect of quick cutting used in film, and can be accomplished with deft lighting and a minimum of props. Think of this piece as a stage documentary of the fictional life of Ira Zimmer.

ZIMMER

Zimmer, a 32-year-old man, in the record store where he works, speaking to a teenage girl.

ZIMMER.   Good album. Excuse me. Good album. Good choice. You should get it. You got any other Doors? Then get it. It's their first. It's good. It's got all their best stuff, like a best-of. "Light My Fire," "The End." You should get it. I know I work here and everything, but if you want my advice, you should go ahead and get it, if you're gonna get any Doors at *all* ... I mean like an intro*duc*tory thing. To *have*. If you like sixties music. If you like sixties music.... Do you? I mean do you have an older brother or something? Yeah? How old is she? Nine*teen*? How old are *you*? I don't know, I thought you were in your twenties at least. Yeah. You're welcome. But if you've got an older sister who's nine*teen* ... you were born in what, '65, '66? No wait, how can that be? Sixty-*nine*? You were born in sixty-*nine*? I was at *Wood*stock in '69. I was in Woodstock and you were in Pampers, I don't believe it. Sixty-*nine*? God I'm getting old. I could be arrested in some states for just talking to you. No. Why, how old do you think I am? How old. Guess. Oh, come on, do I look forty? I know I said I was old, but do I look *forty*? Of course not. I've still got my hair. Guys by the time they're forty.... So you're, what, 18? Ah. Seventeen and a half. Whew. *(Smiles to himself.)* Nothing. Just smiling. So if you're seventeen and a half ... let's see, I'm less than twice your age. No not 36. Less than twice your age. If you're seventeen and a half, and I'm *less than* twice your age, how old am I? No, come back. What's the matter? 'Who's giving you a math lesson? Nobody's giving you a math lesson, we're talking. Okay? Okay? I'm 32. Almost 33. Yeah, that's less than twice your age. 32. Jesus isn't that unbelievable. To me it is, to me it's *un*believable. 32 years old ... *(Shudders, sighs, sadly.)* Anyway, this album. This album is a must if you're starting a sixties collection. I mean if you *were*. They were good, The Doors in the beginning, really good, really special. Great sound. Ahead of their time. When they first came out.... Yeah, he died. Like twenty-something. Can you imagine Jim Morrison alive today? Jim Morrison in his forties? Never. If he were alive today, he would've been dead by now. *(A beat. Sings, à la Morrison a song such as "The End."*)*   •

(Lights shift. A beat.)

(To the audience.) Call me Zimmer. Z-I-double M-E-R. My first name is Ira, but no one calls me Ira. Only people who don't know me very well call me Ira. My *moth*er did and my father did. And my sister and my grandmother. My sister *still* calls me Ira, *when* she calls me.

(A beat.)

ZIMMER'S SISTER. *(While breastfeeding.)* I look at my kids, Ira, and I see you. Look at Gregory. Don't you see you? I do. I'm old enough to remember, you know. I remember when Mommy and Daddy brought you home in the Olds. I waited outside with Bubba on Ocean Avenue, watching the traffic, waiting for Daddy's car. The burgundy Olds. I loved that car. It smelled like French's mustard 'cause of that picnic it spilled. I sat on her lap watching every single car. There it was, turning the corner of Avenue W. Bubba held my hand but I was jumping up and down. I got my baby brother! I got my baby brother! This kvetchy pink roast beef in a blue fluffy blanket. Daddy picked me up so I could see you. Mommy couldn't bend. I remember everything. I have memories from

---

* See Special Note on copyright page.

the *crib* practically. *(Her baby nibbles on her.)* Ow, easy, Gregory. That's Mommy's nipple. You *like* Mommy's nipple. He gets so carried away.

(A beat.)

THE ACTOR. *(To the audience.)* Ira Mitchell Zimmer was born three weeks prematurely, on August 22, 1954, in Monticello, New York. Zimmer's mother's water broke while playing mah jongg at Katzen's Bungalow Colony. Zimmer's parents grew up in East Flatbush within five blocks of one another and attended Samuel J. Tilden High School. They knew each other by sight but never spoke. Years later, Zimmer's mother would enjoy pointing to the photo of the Radio Club in her high school yearbook in which Red Zimmer is in the last row, second from the right, and Estelle is in the third row, dead center, looking just like Linda Darnell, the movie star. Red Zimmer joined the Marines but missed participating in the Normandy invasion when he got drunk during a weekend leave, stumbled, and badly shattered several metatarsal bones in his left foot. He was sent home, where he never revealed the true nature of his wartime injury. Back in Brooklyn, in uniform and on crutches, Zimmer's father was treated like a hero. His family took him out to eat at Lundy's to celebrate his return, where he ran into the girl from high school who looked like Linda Darnell. Struck by the girl's beauty and, playing off her sympathy, he asked her out. They dated regularly for over a year. At the same time, Red was having sex with an Irish girl named Peggy every Thursday afternoon in her Stuyvestant Town apartment, following Red's whirlpool therapy for his injured foot. Caught up in the euphoria after the Japanese surrender, Red drunkenly asked Estelle to marry him. They honeymooned at Niagara Falls during a blizzard and couldn't see a thing. Estelle suffered a miscarriage on New Year's Eve 1948, but went on to have two children, Carol Ann, born May 10, 1949, and Ira Mitchell, whose birth interrupted a mah jongg game five years later. Zimmer's grandmother:

(A beat.)

ZIMMER'S GRANDMOTHER. *(While unwrapping a candy.)* I remember your bris. The screams through the house. The blood. So much blood. Your poor little schvantz, clipped like a chicken at the butcher's. What blood! Your cousin Iris threw up. She was too young. I told them so. Too much excitement. The wine, the flashbulbs. The gefilte fish. The blood.

(A beat.)

ZIMMER, AGE 5. *(Crying.)* I made him bleed, Mommy! This boy Richie! I made him bleed! We were in the pool and I bunked him! I bunked his face and his nose started bleeding! He cried! 'Cause of me! I bunked him! With my elbow! I'm sorry! The counselor Mark made us get out of the pool! We had to stop playing in the water! Richie's blood got in the water and everybody had to get out! 'Cause of me! There was red in the water!

(A beat.)

THE ACTOR. Richie Feldman and Zimmer soon became best friends. Richie was small, fat, and seamy. Brooklyn's answer to Jack Ruby. He compulsively chewed on his knuckles until they were raw and bloody. His parents sent him to a doctor who wrapped gauze around his thumbs. When Richie chewed *through* the gauze to get to his skin, the doctor brushed Mercurochrome on his knuckles so that when Richie chewed on himself, his tongue would sting and his lips would turn orange. Richie masturbated in math class. His classmates got used to the sound of his fist rhythmically smacking the metal underside of his desk during quizzes. Richie had a sister named Bonnie who invented anorexia in the early sixties. His mother, a recluse, remained unseen by friends for years. She was a muffled voice demanding quiet from the next room, a disembodied hand serving milk and Malomars through a darkened doorway. His father sold Israel Bonds.

(A beat.)

ZIMMER, AGE 8. *(During an air raid drill.)* Take cover! *(Covers his head, gets under his school desk giggling, playing with Richie.)* Oh no! It's the end of the world! *(Makes exploding sounds.)* We're all gonna die, Richie!, we're all gonna die! *(More sounds.)* Shh, shh. She's coming. Shh. *(Giggles nervously as the teacher approaches. A beat. To the teacher.)* Nothing. We were just — I know. I know this is serious. *(Shrugs.)* 'Cause it could happen. Khrushchev could press the button and bomb Brooklyn, and then President Kennedy would have to push *his* button and bomb Moscow. And then we'd all be dead, the whole world. But what I don't understand is what difference does it make if we're quiet if we're gonna die anyway? So what if we laugh? It's not like the Russians'll *hear* us. I mean, they know we're here, it's not like we'll be giving ourselves away. Okay, we'll be quiet. We'll be quiet. *(A beat. Zimmer watches as the teacher walks away. He looks at Richie and cracks up, then makes a final exploding sound.)*

(A beat.)

THE ACTOR. *(Reading a composition.)* "P.S. 254, Class 4-209, November 26, 1963. *The Saddest Day of My Life,* by Ira Zimmer. Friday, November 22nd, nineteen hundred and sixty three A.D., was the saddest day of my life. John Fitzgerald Kennedy, the youngest president of the United States of America, was assassinated in Dallas, Texas.

"They let us out of school early but everyone was sad. When I got to our building, all the mothers were outside. Many of them were crying. Nobody could believe that John F. Kennedy was dead and that Vice President Lyndon B. Johnson was now the 36th President of the United States.

"John F. Kennedy was so young and healthy. Who would ever have thought that he would die before the older Mr. Johnson?

"John F. Kennedy was like an uncle or a father you could be really proud of. He was smart, funny, and good-looking, with a beautiful wife of French origin and two cute children, Caroline and John Jr., also known as John-John. John F. Kennedy made people feel good about the future. Now he is no more. I wish I could wake up and find out that the saddest day of my life was something I dreamt, but I don't think so because I believe that I am awake."

(A beat.)

ZIMMER.   *(To the audience.)* When strangers call me Ira, it takes me a second to realize that they're talking to me. I don't correct them. I don't say, "Call me Zimmer" to just anyone. All my teachers called me Ira. Mr. Giordano, who I had for English in the tenth grade, called me Zimmer, but then he used to turn me on in his van in the teacher's parking lot, and we'd quote from Dylan and Ginsberg. He called me Zimmer but I never called him anything. My bar mitzvah teacher, Mr. Klein, he called me Yitzak.

(A beat.)

MR. KLEIN.   No, no, no. Yitzak. Will you never get this right? I'm wasting my breath on you. I tell you, day after day: Practice!, play your record and practice, but you don't listen. How do you expect to get through your bar mitzvah? A miracle? No. No miracles for spoiled boys. This is very funny to you. Laugh, go ahead, laugh. Get used to the sound. There'll be a lot of laughter when you get up in shul to recite your haftorah and nothing comes out of your mouth! For thousands of years Jewish boys have been able to do it except you. How does it feel? Hm? What is so important? Tell me: what is so important, more important than learning your haftorah, What. Baseball? Beatles? Rock and roll? You may as well get up there and *announce,* announce to the congregation, "I have nothing but contempt for each and every one of you!" *(Begins to cough.)* Oh, you are an unworthy boy. Unworthy of manhood. Unworthy of living the kind of life you live. So free. So spoiled. You're no better than my son, may he rest in peace. I thought you were different. You started with such promise. A nice face. A sweet voice. You have the brains. But already you're lost! Lost, and so young, so young. *(Coughing gets worse; breathing becomes difficult.)* I'm old. I'm old and it's hot, and there's plenty of things I'd rather be doing than eating my kishkas out over a spoiled boy in a hot room. You're a *shanda.* For *this* six million died?! So a spoiled boy in Brooklyn should make a mockery?! For *this?!* *(He's stricken; realizes he's having a heart attack.)* Oh, my God ... Yitzak ... Ira ... get help ... please ... don't stand there, help me! God will punish you! *(He falls. A beat. Zimmer, 12 years old, watches in horror and fascination.)*

(A beat.)

THE ACTOR. Summer, 1969. Zimmer is a junior counselor at Camp Shalom in upstate New York. On the night of August 15th, Richie Feldman shows up and coerces Zimmer into going AWOL and coming with him to the Woodstock Music and Art Fair. The following night, while Richie and Zimmer revel in the mud and the music, Zimmer's parents are in Long Island, attending the wedding of his cousin Iris. While driving home from Leonard's of Great Neck, Zimmer's father, feeling the effects of four whiskey sours, plus a champagne toast to the bride and groom, loses control of his Dodge Polara and hits a freezer truck carrying Dolly Madison ice cream. Zimmer's mother is killed instantly. The Van Wyck Expressway is shut down for six and a half hours, causing massive delays. The melted ice cream alone creates a terrible nuisance. Zimmer's father suffers multiple fractures and bruises, and is hospitalized way the hell out in Jamaica, Queens. Broken and depressed like Montgomery Clift, Zimmer's father returns to work at his liquor store in early November, keeping long hours to avoid going home. At one-thirty on the morning of Thanksgiving Day, a 13-year old black kid panics during a holdup and Zimmer's father is shot and killed. On January 2, 1970, cousin Iris's marriage is annulled.

(A beat.)

ZIMMER. John F. Kennedy was in it, I remember *that*. We was walking around and talking and everything, but most of his head was missing. I knew it was John F. Kennedy, though. You know how it is in dreams?, when you *know* something even though it doesn't look absolutely like what you know it's supposed to be? Like, this man, John F. Kennedy, could very well have been my father, who right around this time was murdered also, but in the dream the man is definitely John F. Kennedy. Maybe he was like an actor playing my father. Anyway, he was really pretty cheerful, considering. He was tan and everything. Smiling. I wondered how he could be in such good spirits, smiling and everything, even though he'd been dead for something like five years at this point and his brain was mostly blown away. So I went up and asked him. He was in our kitchen. Of our old house, before my mother died and then my father, before me and my sister had to move in with my grandmother. Oh, *I* remember now: There were these workmen in the kitchen in my dream, hacking away at the walls. There was plaster dust everywhere. They were destroying my mother's kitchen! And there were these three big, elderly black women in flowered house dresses. Three of them, cooing and clucking at one another like a trio of pigeons. I couldn't understand what they were saying. But one of them, she had her glasses hanging on a string around her neck, and she picked them up and looked at me and smiled sympathetically. For some reason, I decided these three black women were like the eternal custodians of our old apartment. It was their job to get it ready for the next tenants, just as they'd done for centuries. I felt very sad, in the dream. And then it was like John F. Kennedy all of a sudden beamed up in the kitchen, wearing his grey, presidential-looking suit, and got himself a beer. *Then* I went up to him and said, "Excuse me, Mr. President, but I can't believe how well you look." "Thank you, Zimmer," he said. He called me "Zimmer!" "I mean, except for the back of your head, you look like you always did. If you didn't turn around, nobody could tell you were dead." And he said, "That's very reassuring. If I could get away with not appearing dead, I'd be a very happy man, indeed." Well, there was every indication that the famous Kennedy wit was in no way impaired by the loss of brain tissue. I was relieved that death doesn't have to destroy one's sense of humor. He made some crack about The Single Bullet Theory, had me in stitches. I couldn't believe that I was standing in my own kitchen with this man who'd meant so much to me my entire life. I tried to tell him, but I couldn't. I started crying. Then he put his arm around me. John F. Kennedy, he had his arm around me. "It's not so bad, Zimmer," he said. "Nothing is lost," he said, "nothing is lost."

(A beat.)

ZIMMER, AGE 15. *(Excitedly.)* Okay, Richie, listen. *(A beat; listening to a record.)* See?! You hear that?! "I buried Paul." That's what John is saying: "I buried Paul." Shit, I'm getting chills. Look at the Sgt. Pepper cover. Look. I mean, come on, what is that? The flowers and the people standing around in the dirt? I mean, where do people stand around in the dirt with flowers all around? A funeral. It's a funeral. I'm not saying it *is* a funeral, I'm saying it *represents* a funeral. It represents Paul's funeral. Laugh all you like, Richie, Paul is dead. The Beatles are finished. God, I'm so depressed. The *Beat*les, Richie. So what if he's not your favorite Beatle? He's not *my* favorite Beatle, either, but still: Paul McCartney, the cute Beatle. It's the end of an era, Richie. They're dropping clues everywhere! "A Day in the Life?": John says, "he blew his

mind out in a car," right? "Don't Pass Me By?" Ringo sings,
"you were in a car crash and you lost your hair." Paul was
killed in a car crash and they didn't want the world to know
because it would be too much. I mean, could you imagine the
hysteria? You saw what Beatlemania was like, can you imagine
dead Beatlemania? Girls would be killing themselves all over
the world! So, they hired this guy who kinda *looked* like Paul,
and gave him plastic surgery, and taught him how to play
leftie. I feel so dumb. I never suspected. Wait, the Abbey
Road cover: Check out the car. What the license plate say?
Un-uh, not 2-8-I-F, 28 IF. Paul would've been twenty-eight *if*
he were alive. Wow, right? Huh? Huh? Unbelievable. Okay,
now listen to the end of "I Am The Walrus" played back-
wards.

(A beat.)

THE ACTOR. 1971. A poem by Zimmer is published in his
high school literary magazine. *(Reads, tongue in cheek.)*
"*The War in My Head,* by Ira Zimmer.
There's this war that's raging in my head,
in black-and-white, non-stop.
Huntley and Brinkley invaded my brain
and don't shut up, they won't shut up.
See, this war in my head
kills my sleep
poisons my dreams
drugs my days.
See, my head aches with all these
noisy dead men crying
But there ain't no Paris peace talks
for this war in my head.
No relief, no aspirin, no secretaries of state.
No, I don't have to go to no Viet Nam
by Army plane and boat and helicopter
'Cause there's this war, see, right here in my head.
That kills my sleep and poisons my days.

And what it's done to my dreams, man,
it just ain't fair.
No, it ain't fair."

(A beat.)

ZIMMER'S SISTER. *(While breastfeeding.)* You and me, we're
very different, Ira, you *know* that. *You* know that and *I* know
that. I think I was put on this earth to have babies. That's
what I do best. It's such a complete and total turn-on for me,
I can't tell you. Being pregnant, nursing. I could come right
now, I swear. *(Giggles.)* If only you could find yourself a girl.
I know, I know, I sound like your mother. Mommy would
never even've said that to you. But a girl, Ira. You gotta try
to hold onto something for a change. You never even tried.
Love, Ira. Babies.

(A beat.)

ZIMMER, AGE 19. *(On the telephone.)* Hello, is Wendy there?
Tell her Zimmer. Zimmer. Ira, yeah. Hi. How come, is she
sick? Look, I'm sure if you told her I was on the phone....
Could you? Could you just tell her it's me, she won't mind
getting out of bed, I promise. Ask her. Give her the choice.
I'm *not* being smart, Mrs. Siegerman.... Thank you. *(To himself.)*
Jesus ... *(Pause.)* You sure your mother doesn't work for the
S.S.? Hi. So what happened?, you were supposed to meet me
at the Fillmore, you okay? You sure?, you sound funny. Yeah,
you do. So where were you? Yeah, I *was* worried, what do you
think? I mean, it wasn't *pleasant* standing there by myself,
thinking I was seeing you every ten seconds. There are so
many Wendy clones with light brown frizzy hair, you would
not believe it. I kept on asking these freaks to hold my place
in line so I could call my grandmother to see if you'd called
to say you were late or dead or something. I decided you *were*
dead. Murdered on the QB. I am *not* morbid. What did you
think I'd think when you stand me up like that?! I mean,
Wendy, come on!, how was I supposed to know you didn't

feel like it? We had so much fun when we waited for Crosby, Stills, Nash and Young, didn't we? Well? Why not The Who? If you didn't really like them.... Don't you even want to know if I got us tickets? Yeah, I did. Don't you want to know *where*? Fifth row. So what's the matter? Don't tell me nothing. What did I do, you're mad at me. Yes you are, why else are you acting so weird? Okay!, so you don't feel well!, what's the matter with you!? *(A beat; nervous smile.)* Yeah, right. *(Long pause; quietly.)* Right there in his office he did it? Did it hurt? *(Pause.)* Why didn't you tell me? I mean, don't you think you should've told me? I mean, I got you into this, you could've *told* me.... No wonder your mother was so ... *(A beat.)* You didn't tell her it was me? It *was* me, wasn't it?, I mean, I *was* the one, wasn't I? I mean, don't I even get credit for *that?* I mean, shit, Wendy, why the fuck didn't you tell me in the first place? You knew all this time and you knew what you were gonna *do* about it and you never even *told* me?! What *am* I to you anyway? *(Pause.)* I'm gonna let you go now. Uh, look, don't worry about the ticket. I'll get Richie or somebody to come with me. So, take it easy, I hope you feel better. Yeah. Bye.

(A beat.)

THE ACTOR. Zimmer drops out of Brooklyn College after one semester and travels cross-country with Richie Feldman. In Las Vegas, Richie tries to persuade Zimmer to share a prostitute with him. Zimmer refuses, they argue, and split up. Zimmer uses all of his pocket money to purchase a Trailways bus ticket. Once back at his grandmother's house in Brooklyn, Zimmer stays in his room for five months.

(A beat. Zimmer, age 20, headphones on, smoking a joint, singing, loudly and off key, a few bars of a song like Bob Dylan's "Like a Rolling Stone."*)

* See Special Note on copyright page.

(A beat.)

ZIMMER'S SISTER. I'm very disappointed in you, Ira, if you want to know the truth. I had high aspirations for you. Ever since you were a little boy. You had such patience. Playing by yourself, making the most beautiful pictures, for hours at a time. You were so quiet, Mommy was always asking if you were okay. You were so fucking talented. You were! I'm not saying I'm jealous, I'm saying you were amazing! There were so *many* things you could do! The music and the art! The poetry in the school magazine! Where did that *come* from, Ira?, the poetry! I thought you'd've been a famous something by now. Thirty-two years old. A famous record producer or something. A David Geffen. I thought you'd've been doing something special with your life. What the hell happened? You were supposed to put the Zimmers on the map. We're not on any map, Ira, we should've been. We're not on any map.

(A beat.)

THE ACTOR. Between 1974 and 1980, Zimmer does the following: enrolls in a night course at Kingsborough Community College in Literature of the Fantastic: From *Lord of the Rings* to *Cat's Cradle*, but attends only four times; sells tie-dyed tee shirts at the Sunrise Drive-in Flea Market for three summers; deals marijuana for eight months, and earns $21,000; sells Amway products and successfully recruits his brother-in-law, who today is an Amway district supervisor; attends a series of Scientology seminars, where he meets Anita Santiago, a junior at NYU, with whom he has sex every Thursday night for ten months; sells car radios at Crazy Eddie; works in the Pop section of J & R Music World; is promoted to assistant floor manager of the Rock 'n Roll department, where he can still be found Tuesday through Saturday. *(A beat.)* On December 8, 1980, after the murder of John Lennon, Zimmer visits Richie Feldman at a drug rehabilitation clinic on the Lower East Side. Zimmer brings a cassette player, a selection of Beatles tapes, and a six-pack of Budweiser. It's their first meeting since going their separate ways in a Las Vegas parking lot seven years earlier. They play all of the tapes, some of them two and three times, drink all of the beer, and reminisce. Richie begins to rant incoherently... *(The actor "becomes" Zimmer.)* ... something about a bloody nose he says I gave him. I thought he was joking at first, and the next thing I knew, he hit me in the head with the cassette player. Richie ran out onto East 9th Street, where he was struck and killed by a Gypsy cab.

(A beat.)

ZIMMER'S GRANDMOTHER. *(While unwrapping a candy.)* It was the drugs. Once that Richie, that boy Richie, started you on the drugs, I could see you disappearing. Fading away. A ghost like all the rest. The smoke of those joints in your room. Constantly, constantly. It got so, my furniture smelled from it. My pillow. The milk in the Frigidaire. It became such a way of life, that even *I* didn't smell it anymore. Who knows, maybe I was stoned myself, breathing the same air all those years. That Richie.... What could I do? An old lady all of a sudden raising two teenagers. The hair, the music, the craziness. What could I do? I ate my heart out from you. What did I know from joints and grass and all that *chazarai?* Uch.... There *is* such a thing as being cursed, you know. My curse was to lose everything I had hope in. My brilliant grandson with the future. What happened to the future, tateleh?, what?

(A beat. Fade up on Zimmer in the record store, as in the beginning of the play, singing the closing lyric of a song like "The End,"* by the Doors.)

* See Special Note on copyright page.

(A beat.)

ZIMMER.   *(To the audience.)* I *am* Zimmer. I am "one who zims." I zim through life. I zim along the surface, the way a good skater zims across the ice. I zim, like the bullets that zim off of Superman's chest, like Hendrix would zim on his guitar. There is no meaning to the verb "to zim"; I give it meaning. *I* zim. I have zimmed, I will continue to zim. I lost Ira somewhere along the way. He just couldn't keep up with my zimming. *(Shrugs.)* I zim. *(Lights fade. Music: The Doors' "The End."*)*

THE END

*   See Special Note on copyright page.

• **TAKI**
greatest
the scrut
moving
politics,
[4M, 3W

• **MIS**
MISSIN(
dramatis
unusual
talk thei
CHRIST

foremost
ley has an
nich people
KISSING

• **THE**
author (
Best Bro
lengthy
Yorker.
cultural
Times. [4

-winning
Award for
ng after a
us." --New
social and
rs." --N.Y.

• **MAST**
Play. O
Terrence
unforget
white-h
theatric

d for Best
mpassion!,
year, an
One of the
"Blazingly

• **DEA**
to gaml
tracks
dissecti
wisecra
charact
York). [

addicted
"... make
zor-sharp
a witty,
nctive ...
Out (New

• **RIF**
one of
effectiv
numbea
vital re
them."

debut of
ingly and
rface of a
ne of the
y they say

440 Park Avenue South, New York, NY 10016 212-683-8960 Fax 212-213-1539
postmaster@dramatists.com www.dramatists.com